JAGUAR
PROJECT XJ40

The Inside Story of the New XJ6

JAG

PROJE

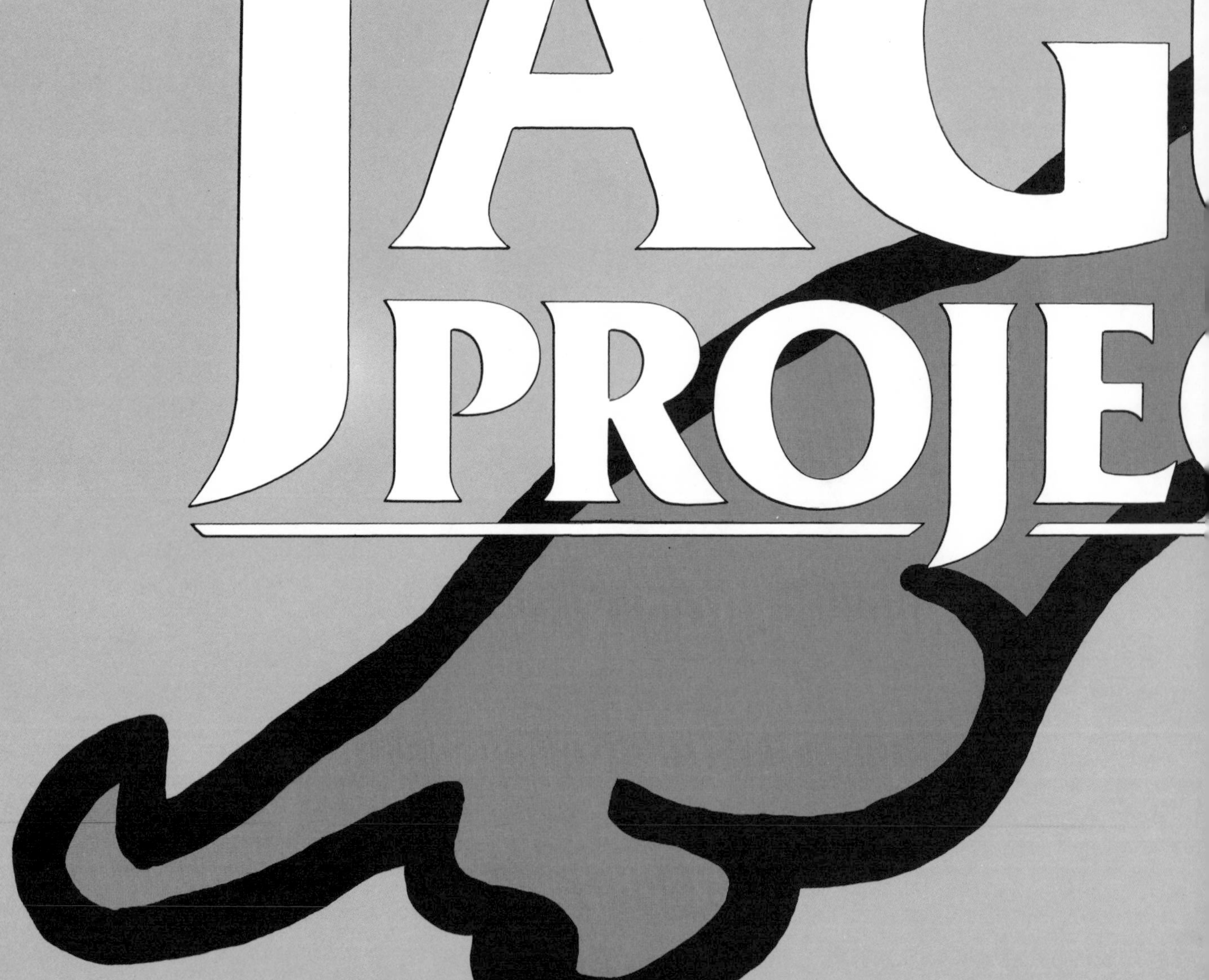

Philip Porter

Foulis

Haynes

ISBN 0 85429 597 6

A **FOULIS** Motoring Book

First published 1987
Reprinted 1987 and 1988

© Philip Porter

Published by:
Haynes Publishing Group
Sparkford, Nr. Yeovil, Somerset
BA22 7JJ, England

Haynes Publications Inc.
861 Lawrence Drive, Newbury Park,
California 91320 USA

**British Library Cataloguing in
Publication Data**
Porter, Philip
   Jaguar project XJ40: the inside story
   of the new XJ6.
   1. Jaguar automobile
   I. Title
   629.2'222   TL215.J3
   ISBN 0-85429-597-6

Library of Congress catalog card number
86-83367

Editor: Mansur Darlington
Page Layout: Mike King
Printed in England, by: J.H. Haynes & Co. Ltd

Contents

1O DOWNING STREET
LONDON SW1A 2AA

THE PRIME MINISTER

The new model Jaguar XJ6 proves Britain's car industry can take the lead in producing a first class car.

The story of its conception, manufacture and marketing is an example of British engineering and enterprise at its best. The ability of our engineers to forge ahead and break new ground will allow us to set the pace for future developments in this field.

Innovation must make a major contribution to the successful future of the car industry. This progressive spirit can be seen in Jaguar's achievement.

The inimitable style and combination of traditional standards with new technology in Jaguar's latest car endorses an enviable reputation.

Quality counts in today's international market place. And this story about British engineering achievement deserves to be told. I extend my best wishes for its success.

Margaret Thatcher

<u>**FEBRUARY 1987**</u>

Introduction

This story is a tribute to many people and I have chosen to tell much of it in the actual words of many of them.

As it is a modern story, full of vitality, I felt it would be more interesting expressed in the words of those involved as they have told it to me, rather than translated into my inevitably impersonal words and the third person. In this way it is genuinely the 'inside story'.

This might appear an easier way of writing a book, indeed even a lazy way. As I have found to my cost, quite the reverse is the case. I have kept the manufacturers of dictaphone cassette tapes in business, have literally worn out several transcribing machines and burnt much midnight oil!

I have lost count of the number of interviews I have conducted in the last three months but I have tried to present a balanced view that is neither a PR handout of excessive magniloquence nor an attempt to find and magnify every problem experienced, and so 'rubbish' the product in typical British fashion. Inevitably there have been one or two inconsistencies in certain accounts but I have, wherever possible, verified my information and I believe the result is a truthful record. I admit it is an optimistic account because optimism seems once again to be totally justified.

The team that faced the eighties inherited a Herculean challenge on all fronts. The company was in deep trouble with components of appalling quality from many large suppliers and catastrophic, suicidal workmanship from another plant within BL. Indeed the company had suffered the dreadful, misguided ravages of BL and its successive managements, taking Jaguar to the brink of extinction, as a company, if not as a name. That it survived the seventies, when many once proud names did not, was a miracle.

The XJ40 tentatively began its long gestation period at the commencement of that decade. Following a brief look at the evolution of the Jaguar saloon from the first unitary construction car and a more detailed look at the remarkable XJ ranges, we trace the early designs intermingled with the politics and turmoil, that are sadly an inseparable part of the story and may serve to explain many of the problems.

We then take a look in some depth at the design and development of the XJ40 from Concept Approval through to finality. There is detail of where the car is particularly innovative, such as the electrical system. There is coverage of the extraordinarily extensive testing and throughout, the story is spiced with anecdotes and amusing or ironic incidents from the men who were, and have been, involved.

Vital though it obviously is, there is very much more to operating an automobile manufacturing company, and launching a new model, than designing and developing the car. For this reason, I have included chapters on the approach to manufacturing, on the reorganisation of the dealer network and the marketing of the new car. Following a chapter on the detailed final specification and my impressions of driving examples in some anger, plus

a look at how the Press reacted, we delve into the 'theatrical' launches whether they be to the trade, the unions, the City, the employees or the public. The concluding chapter is one of reflections, a glimpse of the future and a lengthy interview with Sir John Egan, chief architect of the charismatic revival.

I have, incidentally, referred to the new car, with few exceptions, as the XJ40, rather than, say 'the new XJ6'. To do otherwise would have been excessively confusing, or unacceptably repetitive. Will it become known, in time, as the Series IV or will the 'XJ40' stick for good? We poor scribblers will need some way of distinguishing the car from its forbears.

Jaguars have always been, and are still, remarkable cars. Before the launch, Jaguar's advertising agency carried out a great deal of research and analysed their findings. From this they perceived the strengths on which to promote the new car. Jaguar could achieve 'engineering perfection', because only Jaguar, apart from the very small specialists, is not a volume car manufacturer. A Jaguar is 'exclusive' because its competitors *are* volume manufacturers.

Jaguar offer, as always, remarkable value, with the XJ6 being the cheapest £16,000 car in the world thanks to the feel, handling and materials of luxury. It is not a £9,000 car with £7,000 of extras included. A Jaguar has 'quality and reliability' being the most tested in its field, and having been driven not only by engineers, but by real people!

The Jaguar car makes corporate commonsense in the business/luxury sector. The Jaguar company is the 'Jewel in the Crown of British Industry'. 'Their success is reflected in the product, as their product is in their success. The philosophy behind the new car is that success comes from excellence, and vice versa.'

One cannot help reflecting that if the nation could apply itself to its problems as Jaguar has done, could work as hard as Jaguar people have and produce such fine products, Britain would be the proudest and greatest nation in the world today.

Philip Porter
Knighton-on-Teme, Worcs.

Acknowledgements

Any author writing an Acknowledgements page has, I think, two main problems. Firstly, it is obviously essential to try to remember everyone who has assisted in whatever way and, secondly, he must find 'fifty' or more ways of saying 'thank you' sincerely but in a readable form. I have these problems in a particularly acute form, both because so many people have helped, but also because so many have given so much time and very kind assistance.

Everyone says it is invidious to single out names – and then proceeds to do so. I am no exception!

Two of the central characters of this story have been two of the most helpful. Bob Knight has spent hours, often way into the night, recalling his experiences, explaining technicalities and reliving the unhappy seventies in which he played such a vital role. It was Bob who set such an engineering standard for his successors to improve on and I am delighted to be able to fully acknowledge his part in the great Jaguar story. Jim Randle, who took over the embryonic project, and has nurtured it to maturity and great success, has enlightened me at length, lent me private photographs, provided hitherto confidential information, given permission for many unseen photos to be published to illustrate the early '40' story and given 'my' project his blessing, thereby opening doors and making life much easier.

Former employees George Buck, Bob Blake, Cyril Crouch, Tom Jones, and Doug Thorpe have all spent time remembering past days with great clarity. Peter Whurr kindly invited me to one of the 'J' Days and Neil Edwards showed me around with great enthusiasm. Colin Holtum and George Thompson went to great lengths to explain the styling exercises of the seventies. In the PR department Arnold Bolton has been most helpful, as ever, and I am grateful to Colin Cook for various assistance.

Peter Scholes told me the fascinating story of the electrics, to say nothing of the electronics, and Malcolm Oliver took me through development and testing, providing much useful information. George Mason gave me a most helpful down-to-earth account of the project and explained all about the 'buggy'. David Crisp, editor of *Topics,* the excellent in-house journal, has been most co-operative. Stuart Spencer has helped in a variety of ways including lending me some of his excellent graphic work and I am indebted to Colin Johnson for telling me about 'Sausage, Peas and Chips'.

With regard to photographs, I have once again been assisted enormously by Roger Clinkscales in the Photographic Department. In spite of it being a desperately busy time for him and his colleagues, he managed to produce a significant proportion of the photos in this book. (The Jaguar Cars photos are credited with the initials JC.) John French and his colleagues at the F. John French Agency have been efficiency personified and John Davies of Cricket Communications kindly found time to provide photos of their dramatic visual work.

John Morgan entertained me with

his splendid anecdotes and I feel the book has benefitted greatly from his fund of stories. In the same department I am grateful to Roger Putnam for a most informative interview and to Robert Collier for taking the time, in spite of a hectic Motor Show stand, to talk about matters. Chris Baker provided much information on the launch. Joe Greenwell took me through the mysteries of market research and Pat Smart, as always, has been a good friend.

I enjoyed all the many, many interviews but none more so than the one with Derek Waelend, though I do not recall saying very much! Mike Beasley was most generous with his time and imparted much useful information. Both these gentleman's secretaries, June Bricknell and Elizabeth Ford, went out of their way to make my task easier, as did a number of other secretaries plus Val King on reception.

I am grateful for the contributions of Mike Kinski, Tom Holmes, Terry Williams, Mike Walker, Trevor Crisp, Michael Hughes and Richard Cresswell, for the much valued assistance of Jonathan Heynes and miscellaneous help from Christopher and Diana Ryan, Chris Picaud and Julian Ghosh. One or two dealers seemed publicity shy and were less than helpful when I requested photographs but Steve Broadhurst of Colliers was quite the opposite and photos arrived almost before I had put the phone down!

I am ever mindful of the important part that Norman Dewis plays in much of my Jaguar writing with his unique fund of experience and excellent memory.

Two people who I believe will get considerable credit in the future for what they have recently done and are doing for Jaguar, though in very different fields, are Geof Lawson and Ken Edwards. Both have shown immense kindness and something I particularly value – trust.

I should like to thank the Editors of the various publications from which I have quoted for permission to do so. In particular I would like to acknowledge Gordon Cruickshank, who I hope is still talking to me, Quentin Spurring, Howard Walker, Mike McCarthy, Steve Cropley and Matthew Carter.

My thanks go to Sir John Egan for his time, pertinent contribution and the kindness he has done me in according me a lengthy interview.

I wish to extend my sincere appreciation to Rod Grainger and Mansur Darlington of Haynes for guidance, support and all manner of assistance. My friends Gordon and Jean Benbow have once again proved what good friends they are, and Rosemary Bird has contributed enormously in every sense as well as keeping me relatively sane.

I am particularly grateful and highly honoured that the Prime Minister, for whom I have enormous respect, has found the time to grace my book with her Foreword.

Publisher's note

Many of the development photographs supplied by Jaguar for use in this book were intended originally for internal reference purposes only. Though some might have been omitted on the grounds of not being of first-rate quality the decision was reached easily that they should be reproduced because of their historical importance and technical interest.

Chapter 1
Jaguar Heritage

The secret of Jaguar success has always been style. It was style that first sold the little Swallow sidecars and the Swallow saloons produced by young Billy Lyons in the twenties. It was style that helped Bill Lyons' growing company through the difficult thirties with the rakish SS's and SS Jaguars. Through the fifties and sixties, style and performance sold the sports cars, first XKs and later E-types, and the saloons produced by Sir William Lyons' growing empire.

More latterly, it has been style, combined with most fortuitous and favourable dollar/sterling currency fluctuations, that has sold the Series III XJ saloons in the United States that resuscitated the company when its life hung in the balance.

Closely allied to this style has been first class, often pioneering, engineering and the justly famous value for money. In the late 1980s nothing has changed. Jim Randle, Engineering Director, might rightly describe his new car as 'a computer on wheels'; but without that essential Jaguar style as

well, it would be just another box like the opposition.

As we shall see, Jaguar looked at other ideas, at other people's ideas, indeed at many ideas, but thankfully returned to a car that is distinctly a Jaguar. This distinction is born of a fine heritage, so before tracing more recent developments, it might be interesting to take a brief look at the company and the evolution.

SS Cars, as the company was known in the thirties, and Jaguar Cars, as it became after the war, was led by a triumvirate of immense significance to the success of the venture. This success demanded expanded facilities and in 1952 Lyons purchased the 1,187,500 square foot former Daimler No.2 shadow factory at Browns Lane for £1 per square foot. William Lyons, as is well known, was the founder (co-founder to be absolutely precise), brilliant stylist and administrator. William Heynes was successively Chief Engineer, Engineering Director and Vice-Chairman,. Arthur Whittaker, rather less known, was the General

Manager.

Apart from managing the business when Lyons was away. Whittaker's area of responsibility was in purchasing all parts that might be called original equipment. Nothing was purchased unless Whittaker had a hand in it and so skilled was he in negotiating that Jaguar bought as, if not more, competitively than anybody in the industry. This was one of the fundamental reasons why Lyons was able to offer such remarkable value for money.

The story is told that when, in 1966, Lyons sold out to BMC and it was announced on the evening news, the suppliers were literally queuing up next morning to ask if there was any way Whittaker could avoid divulging his component prices to BMC because Jaguar were buying them cheaper!

As an example, a 5 inch speedo was being bought for 35 shillings by the British Motor Corporation and by Jaguar for under 30 shillings!

The story of Jaguar's racing exploits is well known with the C and D-type's five Le Mans wins; the myriad national

and international racing and rallying successes with XK120s and the big saloons; the total domination of touring car racing by the small saloons; and, more recently, further success with XJS's and Jaguar engined sports racing cars, to name just a few. The Le Mans wins, above all, put Jaguar on the international map and was money very well spent. The boost to the image and the pride engendered in the workforce are intangibles, but it is interesting to reflect that Jaguar is probably the only British manufacturer of production cars ever to have made money out of motor racing.

Bill Heynes was a great racing enthusiast and Lyons was a shrewd businessman. The involvement had the added advantage of creating a superb team of engineers who applied the lessons learnt on the track to the road cars. This team included such men under Heynes as Bob Knight, Malcolm Sayer, Phil Weaver and Norman Dewis. Lofty England, the Service Director, having previous competition experience, took charge of the racing team. As to drivers, just about anybody who was anybody has at one time or another raced or rallied Jaguars.

The roots of the XJ40 go back to the little 2.4-litre saloon announced in 1955. Significantly it was the first Jaguar to abandon the chassis and instead have a stressed body of unitary construction. The front suspension was mounted on a separate sub-frame with coil springing and top and bottom wishbones. In broad principle this set-up has continued to the present, particularly the important rubber mounting.

This model was the first Jaguar to have a curved windscreen, and Bob

Knight, who was in charge of vehicle development, recalls Lyons, who always addressed everybody by their surname, described the shape as 'rotund style, you know, Knight'!

Knight feels that the car 'was a landmark in the development of the Jaguar unitary construction with comparatively good road and mechani-

> The 2.4 saloon had the distinction of being the first unitary construction car to be produced by Jaguar and the evolution which culminated in the XJ40 can be traced back to this first 'compact' model. (J.C.)

cally excited noise. In its early form it was like a van – a really dreadful thing. It was necessary to develop the whole set of mounting systems, like the front and rear suspension, the engine and transmission. All had to be radically rehashed in development to achieve the acceptable levels of silence and smoothness.

'Our roots of understanding the business of refining motor cars go back to this model.'

With overdrive fitted, the car was capable of 100 mph and at £1269, including purchase tax, was remarkable value for money. Its narrow live axle, however, just 4 ft x 2½ in, detracted from stability, and, more importantly, the American market, at which this sporting compact was aimed, demanded more straight line power.

This demand was satisfied by the introduction of the more usual 3.4 version of the legendary XK engine in the same bodyshell. One now had an 120 mph car with those famous Jaguar characteristics: good torque and low speed flexibility. Whilst the braking now caused concern, the car could

> The Mark 2 saloon produced with 2.4, 3.4, and 3.8-litre engines was a considerably improved car and was often described as the 'businessman's express'. (J.C.)

achieve 19 mpg, and customers had the option of automatic transmission. By today's standards the handling and cornering are somewhat dated to say the least but the performance is still very respectable.

Disc brakes, developed by Dunlop for aircraft use and then by Jaguar for cars, and initially used on the racing C and D-types with devastating effect, were adopted on the 3.4 saloons in late 1957 and the braking now matched the performance.

The appearance of the car was considerably improved with the introduction, in October 1959, of the evolutionary Mark 2 model. More slender roof pillars, a larger rear window and chrome window frames contributed to this, with a wider rear axle aiding stability. The 2.4 and 3.4 models were joined by a 3.8-litre version which gave 125 mph and a 0-60 time of 8.5 sec whilst still returning 19 mpg. Not surprisingly this model was very popular in the States.

Indeed, the whole range was important to the growing company with a little under 100,000 Mark 2s being produced over the years. Whilst the sports cars always contributed to the dramatic image and also usefully to the coffers, it was always the saloons that were the volume earners.

For £3m Lyons purchased the Daim-

ler company in 1960 and acquired, apart from a diverse range of vehicles, another factory thereby doubling the floor space. Prior to this cars were being made at the rate of up to 500 per week at Browns Lane and the gross profit to assets employed ratio was 68%.

In 1961, a few months after the unleashing of the E-type, the company announced the Mark X saloon. At 16 ft 10 in long with a width of 6 ft 4 in, it was massive. The very bulbous, and now very dated, body was influenced by the US market where it was greeted initially with a mixed reaction. It was very heavy at 37 cwt and there were early production and quality problems, but the concept was advanced for such a large car. It never, however, sold in the intended numbers.

Of more lasting significance the car featured the new independent rear suspension first seen on the E-type. This suspension, which was the result of a bet between Lyons and Knight in 1958, and designed and fitted to a 3.4 by Knight in 27 days to win the bet, was to be fitted to every new model until the XJ40. Again, the employment of rubber mountings gave the car the high levels of road insulation and low noise that Jaguar's have become famous for. In spite of its size, the Mark X drove well with a top speed of 120 mph but, not surprisingly, the consumption worked out at between 13 and 17 mpg dependent on conditions or driving style.

The introduction in 1964 of the enlarged 4.2-litre engine gave the car extra torque and the model was gradually improved. A year earlier the existing range had been supplemented by a new model, the S-type. It was, in appearance, a Mark 2 with a Mark X tail and independent rear suspension. Available in 3.4 and 3.8 forms, it was highly rated by the Press who considered it more modern than the Mark 2's and more practical than the Mark X.

Bob Knight recalls that in the mid-sixties Heynes was keen to build a V12 engine and the mid-engined XJ13

to go racing and Lyons wanted to produce a large limousine. A meeting took place between the two in the middle of the Experimental Shop and it was agreed that Heynes could have his racing car if Lyons could have his limousine!

In the mid-sixties we were, therefore, developing the XJ6, the limousine and the XJ13. Lyons felt, however, that the XJ6 was not going to be announced soon enough so then came the saga of the 420.

In late 1965 Lyons became convinced that a further modification to the S-type was required in order to live.

So he re-worked the front end and went to Pressed Steel Fisher stating that he wanted it in production by next July even thought at that stage there were no tools, or even drawings! The two most senior executives of PSF thought this was a good joke and said it was quite out of the question. No amount of persuasion would succeed and Lyons, who was a man who, if he was determined to have blue roses and

there was no other way of getting them, would have them sprayed, said, 'All right, if you won't do them, I'll have the first 2,000 sets made by hand'!

In the end PSF gave in and actually drew it, tooled it and got the first bodies off tools in July. That, I should think, was the worst six months of their working lives, but that was Lyons' way of doing things. He would never let anything stand in the way of what he was convinced he needed.

So in October 1967 Jaguar took a further step nearer the XJ concept with the introduction of the 420. This was essentially an S-type with the Mark X type front body treatment and, as the name implied, the 4.2 engine. John Morgan, Export Manager at the time, recalls that the Americans, and a lot of the Europeans, did not like the S-types, 'but as soon as we put the different grille on, it went immediately'.

With increased torque it was a more pleasant car to drive than the S-type and the *Autocar* commented that the 420, 'for a combination of speed, comfort and safety is as good as any in the world, regardless of cost.' By this time, however, the shape was becoming rather dated and, furthermore, some rationalisation was needed for the company was producing the 240 and 340 – as the Mark 2s had become known – 3.4 and 3.8 S-types, open two-seater, fixed head and 2 + 2 E-types, the 420 and 420G, as the Mark X had been renamed, to say nothing of the left-hand drive and

> The enormous Mark X saloon now looks very dated with its great bulbous sides but it looked a fine car in its day and one can see the XJ shape beginning to form in Sir William's mind. (J.C.)

market variations. The Daimler 2½-litre V8 engine had been fitted in the Mark 2 body and there were still several Daimler models in low volume production. 'From an engineering point of view,' states Knight, 'this was all terribly indigestible'.

In fact the company was to alter course dramatically going from a profusion of models to just one saloon concept.

Before going on to look at the development of the XJ4, that became known as the XJ6 when introduced in 1968, it may be interesting to touch on a few of the projects and experiments carried out over the years on the cars so far described. Many of these will probably be unknown to readers and give some background to Jaguar thinking. As facts come to light they either explain or confuse!

It may, however, be interesting to see just when Jaguar started on the various models that did appear. Clearly, as cars became more sophisticated, development intensified and gestation periods extended.

Although the first production Jaguar to feature a unitary construction body was the 2.4 saloon, the Experimental Dept did, in fact, build an 'integral chassis/body construction' Mark VII saloon. It was listed amongst the

experimental cars in August, 1957 but the lack of a chassis number probably indicates that it was never run.

The same 1957 list yields the information that a black convertible 3.4-litre had been constructed and that already Jaguar were playing with a wide rear track on a 3.4 By July 1958 the same car had been fitted with fuel

> The 420 took the S-type concept a stage nearer the XJ shape with revised front-end styling and was a slimmer version of the Mark X, which had by now become known as the 420G. (J.C.)

injection and a 2.4 was referred to with a 'wrap-around windscreen' plus a 3.4 with restyled body. This is probably the first Mark 2. The same year the third 3.4 made was running with Knight's independent rear suspension and a similar car, registered TVC 420, which had previously been listed with light alloy doors, was now fitted with a 3.8 engine.

The 'wrap-around' car and convertible were sadly scrapped but by July 1960, there was a curious reference to a 'Mark II body shell for modification to GT type' and a 3.8 with restyled boot. A 3.4, which was later fitted with a

Daimler SP250 engine, was listed as having 'air suspension'.

By December 1960 three Zeniths, the code name for the Mark X, had been built and a 3.8 Mark 2 fitted with air conditioning. Eighteen months later the first prototype Mark X had been fitted with the 4½-litre V8 Daimler engine, and incidentally proved rather better than the 3.8 XK unit, and a further Mark X had been built with a lightweight

> Insert: The S-type was a happy compromise of Mark 2 styling with the added benefit of independent rear suspension and an enlarged boot. (J.C.)

body. Excellent though the 4½ V8 was, the way it had been designed precluded it from being made in volume.

The records then refer to the first two Mark 3's. By April 1963, the first Mark X had been fitted with a 4.2 engine and the model was given the codename, XJ5. Two months later, the Mark 3's had become Mark 2 S models, obviously the S-type, also known as XJ3!

A 'Mark X Chrysler car' (fitted, it seems, with a Chrysler transmission) is

This is presumed to be the 'Mark 2 GT type' referred to in the list of experimental cars which was merely a mock-up and never ran. (J.C.)

listed in 1964 and by December the following year, XJ5 No.5 had been fitted with a V12 engine, No.4 had been 'prepared to receive V12 engine' and No.6 was running on Lucas fuel injection. Furthermore the Mark 2 S, 3339 KV, had a 4.2 unit and the first three XJ16's (420's) had been built, the last with a 'Daimler grille, etc.'. The same list mentions XJ4 No.1.

There is also reference to a Mark X with Badolini transmission and a Mark 2 2.4 fitted with a 3-litre engine. Another engine comes to light In June 1967. Beside a particular 3.4 Mark 2 there is the comment: 'project to convert to 2.6L when engine is ready'. Around this time two distinguished former Jaguar engine men and close friends, Wally Hassan and Harry Mundy, were running S-types with 4.2 engines installed.

This is just a selection of the projects the company was involved in during the period and makes one realise why the small team struggled to cope with the workload and the decision was made to pull out of racing to concentrate on production cars. It further underlines the need for some rationalisation.

Here we see the same car with fabric laid on the roof to give the appearance of a convertible. Fred Gardner, in spite of his height, shows how low the car was. (J.C.)

Chapter 2
Lyons' Pride

In 1966 a momentous event occurred which was to have consequences of almost catastrophic proportions. Lyons, founder, Chairman and majority shareholder, sold out to BMC. He could not have known at the time but by doing this he was to involve Jaguar in a 'dark age' of corporate financial failure and recurring administrative change.

With this so-called merger, was formed British Motor Holdings. Sir George Harriman, Chairman of BMC, and thus of BMH, had promised a 'hands-off' policy: he was as good as his word and for two years all was well with no interference from the giant corporation. Then Leyland acquired BMH: the formation of the gargantuan British Leyland was the beginning of troubled times for all therein.

Politics and strife dominated the course of events at Jaguar for most of the next 18 years. Only the determination of a few people within Jaguar kept the company in business.

The XJ4, which later came to be known as the XJ6, was to be, in its various guises, the most important Jaguar yet. Sir William had decided to rationalise to such an extent that he would have only one saloon concept and that the fortunes of the company would rest on this one car in various forms. It was a brave decision and a reversal of a policy which had seen, for one reason or another, the company producing so many models and variants.

Whether it was the correct decision or not, there is no denying that the company is still in business, is making money, has only recently replaced the XJ6 some eighteen years later and has been so anxious about following such a superb car.

The six and twelve-cylinder-engined XJs have had every possible accolade accorded them, not only upon announcement, but during their unintentionally long life. If proof were needed of the car's greatness, it is simply given. At the beginning of their lives, each won the coveted 'Car of the Year' award. Even at the end of the Series III XJ6's life, Jaguar could not make

enough to satisfy demand in this fiercely competitive sector of the car market.

The XJ4 project had certainly started in 1964. During the July holiday Bob Knight and Tom Jones, Chief Chassis Designer, started the first suspension schemes. In November Lyons released a full size softwood model of the body style, which was to become so famous, for body engineering and tooling at Pressed Steel Fisher.

At this time the Engineering and Production departments were involved, to their cost, with the very diverse range of existing vehicles and it was felt that one objective of the XJ4 design should be to establish front and rear suspension assemblies and a general layout which could be used across a whole range of future cars. This was done by first establishing a front and rear track dimension that would satisfy this objective. History shows that this aim was eventually achieved.

Records reveal that a lightweight Mark X had been doctored 'to simulate

XJ4 condition' and the first prototype XJ4 was running in May 1966. By the end of 1966, No. 1, a Warwick Grey coloured car, had been joined by the light green No. 2 and black No. 3. A great deal of credit for the brilliant design of the XJ4 should go to Bob Knight who in 1963 had been promoted by Heynes to Chief Vehicle Engineer and Deputy Engineering Director.

Former apprentice David Fielden, who was to become Quality Director in 1978, was the development engineer immediately concerned. A little later Jim Randle was recruited from Rover in a similar capacity.

In a report dated 20 February 1967 Knight summarised the position of the principal development features. 'Three cars are now running and the first and second will be used for most of the outstanding work. The second car will be involved in development of the air conditioning system.'

Under the heading of 'Handling Characteristics,' he stated, 'directional stability and 'feel' now reasonable, and can be varied to taste'. He found that these characteristics were mainly affected by, 'front and rear wheel alignments, stiffness of front lower wishbone bearings and stub axle carrier, transverse stiffness of IRS mountings, rack mounting stiffness, 185 x 15 tyres less sensitive than 195 x 15 inch squat ones, also have heavier feel due to higher pneumatic trail. It will obviously take some time to evaluate the best combination of the above factors, and the engine must now be mounted on the crossmember to establish the final picture.'

Steady state cornering and roll were said to be quite good. 'Roll is rather greater than desired with present 5/8 in roll bar. Front to back balance fairly good with 4.2-litre engine, but it would be better with 11/16 in diameter bar for 3-litre engine. The best all-round job would probably result from the use of a rear anti-roll bar, as on the E-type, but extra expense and complication would be involved.'

A certain amount of development work had already been carried out, and continued to be carried out, on modified Mark Xs. For the new model it was intended that the only six-cylinder unit would be a 3-litre one as it was assumed that this 185 bhp engine would be quite sufficient for the lighter new car. The engine, however, did not possess the traditional Jaguar bottom-end torque and therefore the 4.2 was adopted dictating alterations to the bonnet to accept the taller engine.

From the start it was planned to fit the V12 engine that was being developed, though at this stage there was

This early rear end derived much from the E-type which was actually styled by Malcolm Sayer with detail work by Sir William. (J.C.)

some indecision as to whether it would be the twin-cam version, built originally with racing in mind, or the later, less complex single-cam unit.

The intention also had been to design a new rear suspension based on usual practice but mounted direct to the body and the first cars were so built.

Returning to Bob Knight's report we learn that with regard to axle noise:

With rear suspension mountings at the present state of development, the only gear

whine which is audible in the car is of unusually high frequency (over 70 mph) and has appeared on two axles of the latest type. There is little doubt that the trouble arises from a resonance of the torque tube, which will be investigated on a test rig.

These noise problems, and a lack of time to cure them, were to prove the death-knell of the new suspension for this model. Under the heading 'Over-run boom – 2500 rpm,' Knight states:

Although this appears to be a simple matter, it is the one about which we know least. Sounding exactly like an exhaust note, it does not emanate from the tailpipe nor is it transmitted through the exhaust mountings.

The engine mountings have not yet had high priority so far with the 4.2-litre engine. In the case of the 3-litre engine, it appeared quite easy to get a satisfactory compromise between smoothness and road-excited shake with the engine mounted on the body.

This has been more difficult with the 4.2-litre engine, but may still be possible. However, in view of the success of the crossmember-mounted engine in the XJ5 [420], work will be concentrated on these lines on the XJ4.

Towards the end of the report Knight

As the XJ theme begins to evolve with a mixture of E-type and Mark X influence, we see that Lyons at one stage was playing with this very Italian treatment of the front end. (J.C.)

makes mention of the 'near-final design of axle unit' yet it was not, as stated, to be adopted. As we shall see, however, many elements of this design reappear again later in the story.

By June 1967 No. 1, fitted with a manual 4.2 engine, had run 8,619 miles and was still being used for general handling development. No. 2 had a 3-litre unit with Model 35 automatic

been used for XJ4 original suspension development. 'Not now running,' reported Phil Weaver, 'as rear suspension partially stripped and no rear brakes (transferred to XJ4/1). Has run 61,325 miles. Body panels distorted at rear where modified. Will require MOT Test if run again'!

John Morgan recalls that Lyons called him and several colleagues down to Wappenbury Hall, Lyons' home, one day and showed them the final car.

The grille was really very bland, it was awful. He said to me, 'Well, what do you think of it? Is that going to be alright for you?'

I said, 'Well, I must say it looks rather like a 1955 Studebaker'.

'What did you say?' he exploded.

I said, 'Well it does, it's that solid front'.

'Right.' he said, 'go away'.

A few days later we were called back to his garage and he opened the door and said, 'I'm not going to do anything more to it'. He had taken every other slat out of the

transmission but had covered only 1,048 miles and No. 3, at 1,277 miles, was being used for air intake and exhaust silence development work with the 3-litre engine fitted with a manual 'box. By now No. 4 had been completed with a 4.2 engine and Model 8 automatic transmission. It had run only 16 miles and was to be used for 'cooling transmission and sound deadening development'.

At this stage an obviously hard working Mark X was sounding rather sad! The car, registered 5437 RW, had

By slicing off the rearmost portion of the tail, Lyons arrived at the familiar rear treatment that was to remain a final feature in refined form. (J.C.)

grille and it made a world of difference to it.
'Now,' he said, 'does it look like a Studebaker?' I said, 'No, Sir William, not at all'!

In September 1968 the XJ6, as the public know the car, was announced and received a rapturous reception. The combination of Lyons' styling and Knight's engineering had produced a world beater. Yet the extraordinary thing was that there was nothing radically new about this Jaguar, apart from the styling. All the mechanical features had been seen before in other models. In the XJ6, however, they had been developed and fine tuned to new standards, and placed in a shell which was another Lyons masterpiece.

The XJ6 simply set new standards in silence, ride and comfort.

The car was announced with the familiar 4.2 engine but also with a 2.8 version of the XK unit because such a size conferred tax advantages in certain European countries. Front suspension was similar to previous models but now was mounted on a box section crossmember again. Anti-dive characteristics were built in by inclining the top wishbone upwards and the lower one downwards. The front sub-frame carried not only the front engine mountings but also the Adwest power-assisted rack and pinion steering.

The brakes were of Girling manufacture with dual lines, tandem master cylinder and, of course, a servo. The roadholding benefitted greatly from the SP Sport tyres especially developed by Dunlop for the car. Knight and his team had very successfully engineered out the inherent radial harshness.

As more had been learnt about monocoque techniques and stressing, the body could be made lighter yet stronger. The front was designed for controlled crushing in the event of a collision. However, the body still consisted of a large number of small panels which needed careful assembly and welding together.

The roadtesters discovered the immediate impressions of uncanny silence and superb ride. These attributes, combined with unrivalled handling, traditional quality and excellent perfor-

Above: The car appears rather shorter even than the eventual swb XJ6 and the bonnet with air scoop seems to slope down more than the final car.

Left: The final shape is certainly emerging but it is interesting what a difference the swage line on the rear wing makes swooping, as it does on this mock-up, almost down to the bumper. Below: The front end is now much more traditional Mark X/420 in its execution and apart from the bulbous grille becoming a flat item, this is very close. (J.C.)

The car was not light at 32½ cwt but as Jaguar engineers have learnt, refinement equals weight and vice versa. At the time, though, a fuel consumption of 15 – 18 mpg drew little comment. The manual version was a little more sprightly and reached 60 mph from standstill in an impressive 8.8 seconds with a top speed of 124 mph.

There were criticisms as you would expect but they were relatively minor grouses. The clutch on the manual

mance led to highly favourable comparisons even with the Rolls-Royce and the Mercedes 600. At £2,397 the most expensive Jaguar, the 4.2 Auto, was less than half the price of the comparable 300SEL Mercedes.

The automatic version was not quite as quick in a straight line as some of its illustrious predecessors but with cat-like roadholding qualities was far quicker on most journeys. And on such journeys passengers could remark the total lack of noise at speed from the wind, engine, road or transmission.

version was over-heavy. The steering was certainly over-assisted and the Americans were unhappy with the old fashioned and confusing dash layout. The heating and ventilating system, never a strong point on a Jaguar, was still lacking, apparently, in the more extreme climates.

Production commenced at 140 per week, climbed to 450 by 1970 and two years later was 650. Sir William had been right – as usual.

John Morgan recalls with amusement an incident at the XJ6 launch. Sir William had not been altogether happy about the adoption of the 4.2 engine and the change in bonnet profile it necessitated, although this decision had been taken in 1967. He expressed his view to Morgan that he felt it had spoilt the appearance of the car.

Originally the bonnet was going to be virtually flat because it fitted the V12 and 2.8 but needed a bulge to accommodate the higher 4.2. They had to change the bonnet later on and it did make a slight difference to the effect of the car. So I said, 'Quite honestly Sir William it just has to be. That 4.2 engine is a good engine and we can't only sell a 2.8. So he accepted it and on the day of the launch he walked around with me quietly. The Press had all jumped on him and all said, 'Bill it's marvellous. Bill you've really done it again.'

He whispered to me, 'Morgan, you know I can't understand it. Nobody's said a word about that engine.'

And I said, 'Well I didn't think they would, Sir William, and we can live with it for two or three years'. That was in 1968!

The year 1972 saw the introduction of the fabulous V12 engine. Jaguar thoughts had turned in the past to a V12 engine to keep the company at the forefront of sports car racing with the added glamour such an engine would engender in a road car. A V8 was considered but as America was the major market there was much to be said for not copying that popular configuration but to be different. Furthermore

there are technical advantages to the V12 which is inherently free of primary and secondary out-of-balance forces. The international competition rules allowed a maximum capacity of 5 litres and this was the natural starting point. A four-cam unit was built first and such an engine was fitted in the machine known by Experimental as 'XJ13 No. 1 car'. This was, of course, the mid-engined racing car that sends every Jaguar enthusiast into raptures.

On 18 October 1965 Norman Dewis, Jaguar's legendary and recently retired Chief Tester, reported on the XJ5 No. 5 fitted with a 5-litre V12. On top gear acceleration the car was very similar to a normal 4.2 car and slightly down on an experimental fuel injection 4.2 car. But from rest it was more impressive and recorded 0-60 in 8.5 seconds as opposed to 10.4 for the carburettor car, and 0-110 in 24.7 against 40.3.

Dewis commented, 'speed recorded through the timing lights was 134 mph with tachometer reading 6,000 rpm. At the end of the straight 6,500 rpm was observed which is equal to 145 mph.' He expressed some reservations about the accuracy of the tachometer and then cooly observed, 'during a second run the car had just passed the timing lights when the engine produced a seizure, disengaging top gear and switching off saved the engine from more serious damage'!

Concluding he noted 'low speed flexibility is very good, it being possible to drive the car at 6 mph in top gear on full throttle'.

The grille is now flat but how ghastly it looks showing how important these, seemingly, little detail touches are in refining a style. (J.C.)

A great deal of testing was done with single-cylinder engines with both a single camshaft flat-head design and a twin camshaft hemispherical layout.

The decision was in favour of the single-cam engine for various reasons. The width of the unit across the cam covers and exhaust manifolds was less, making fitment in a confined space rather easier and allowing optimum

savings. Finally there was more space between the vee for auxiliaries. It has also been suggested that the single-cam-per-bank engine gave better low down performance.

Examples of XJ10, as the XJ12's were confusingly codenamed, were running well before the six-cylinder car was launched. The intention was to use Brico fuel injection which showed significant advantages in cold running and maximum power, but Brico cancelled plans to produce the equipment. Jaguar therefore reverted to a carburettor set-up. Interestingly though, a fuel injected twin-cam unit in an XJ10 recorded a standing $1/4$ mile figure of 15.5 seconds in February,

1967 which the production car could not quite match when announced five years later.

The change to carburettors delayed production manufacture of the power unit because of the need to get good mixture distribution and warm-up. This in turn delayed tooling of the inlet manifold and water outlet system. The cylinder block, cylinder head, and other tooling were ready in 1970 but announcement of the XJ12 was not possible until 1972.

Finally, in July of that year the XJ12 was launched to an ecstatic welcome. An unfortunate three month strike only served to lengthen the already daunting waiting lists. Indeed Jaguar's advertis-

wheel lock with the increasingly wide tyres. The head design was simpler and therefore cheaper to produce. There was a weight saving of 26 lb per head and a single chain with four sprockets could be used rather than four chains and twelve sprockets. This obviously saved money and showed weight

Having arrived at a final shape it was camouflaged and several examples were put through their paces to develop the mechanical aspects of the original XJ6s. (J.C.)

ing agency even capitalised on this by commissioning a series of cartoons joking about the rarity of the car.

Apart from the grille the external appearance was very similar to its six-cylinder brother. Ventilated discs assisted the heavy car to stop efficiently and repeatedly, and the magnificent engine drew praise from every quarter. In spite of the insatiable demand the XJ12 was priced very competitively at

With the launch of the XJ6 in 1968, the reaction and orders proved that Lyons, Heynes and Knight had really got it right and the superb, clean styling has stood the test of time together with the exemplary road manners and utter refinement. (J.C.)

The rear treatment is seen here in its final form. The basic XJ shape, with two revisions, was to carry the fortunes of the company through the troubled seventies and into the happier eighties. (J.C.)

£3,725. A Daimler version called the Double Six joined the stable as did an even more luxurious model, the Vanden Plas, which significantly had a four inch longer wheelbase. This gave more rear legroom and improved rear compartment accessibility. The price in September, 1972 was £5,363.

The performance for such a big car was sensational with 60 mph reached from standstill in just 7.4 seconds. Top speed was around 140 mph but consumption at just 11.4 mpg reflected the performance and weight. This level of performance was achieved in remarkable silence even by Jaguar standards and it was difficult to know one was moving, let along quickly.

Long wheelbase versions of the XJ6 and XJ12 were shown at the 1972 Motor Show. These were firstly additional models but later the swb versions were dropped altogether. Ventilation remained poor and, partly due to the need to have light steering effort for the US market, the power

steering still lacked feel. *Motor* magazine unfavourably compared the Jaguar to the Aston Martin, in this respect, and I clearly remember the excellent DBS and unpleasant XJ, having owned examples of both some years later.

In May 1973 the 2.8-litre version, after a troubled life, was dropped. John Morgan was particularly disappointed with the problems.

> With the British Leyland influence starting to hamper Jaguar, it took four years to introduce the V12-engined version but, when the XJ12 finally appeared, it was heralded as one of the world's great cars – some would say the greatest. (J.C.)

It was such a pity because that car could have got us big volumes. It was in the right tax category all over Europe and benefitted from cheaper insurance. That was why Mercedes kept making a 2.8 for so many years. I would have liked us to have produced a 2.8 swb and a 4.2 lwb. My great hope had been that we would be able to compete with BMW and Mercedes in 1968 and of course we never did. So we lost five years or more.

Jaguar could have been up to 55,000 plus production by the early seventies if that car had been a good car. Even with the BL mess-up the dealers were still strong enough in 1969/70.

As thoughts began to form for an XJ6/12 replacement, as we shall see, Jaguar launched the Series II at Frankfurt in September 1973. The engineers had addressed themselves to the areas of criticism and certain revisions were forced by the 1974 US regulations. To meet these the bumper was raised to a height of 16 inches and the grille was, therefore, now split with a shallower grille above the bumper and a rectangular one below. Many felt then, and still do today, that the front was improved by these enforced changes.

The rear end was only altered by the moving of the number plate lamp from the bumper to the boot lid lip so that it shone down rather than up. US export cars additionally had the first of the ghastly black rubber 5 mph impact bumpers grafted onto the normal

blades with extra flasher lamps on the sides of all four wings.

The heating, ventilating and optional air conditioning systems were completely redesigned and improved. This necessitated some redesigning of the front bulkhead. Particular attention was paid to sound deadening and heat sealing this bulkhead, the front of which was covered by asbestos and the rear by Hardura PVC foam and oilfield bitumen and felt. Conventional rubber grommets were eliminated and instead multi-pin sockets were affixed to each side of the bulkhead wall and wiring was connected via plugs.

Subsequent tests by General Motors of the new air conditioning system showed that its performance was comparable to good American practice.

The dash layout was considerably revised to satisfy US criticism and certain functions became controlled by column mounted stalks rather than the previous confusing plethora of identical rocker switches.

John Morgan remembers that a number of problems were ironed out on the Series II models such as bad petrol smells and interior heat.

When the first one came out, I had one down in the South of France, bringing it back from Italy, and I had two ladies in the back. Suddenly they asked, 'what are you trying to do with us? Every time you go over a slight bump, we get a shaft of hot air up our back sides!'

The thing was so hot underneath, I told Lofty, everything melted in the boot. If you had clothes in a case in the boot, they were all pressed by the time you got to your house! The heat under the car was running along and over the back axle. Therefore as soon as the rear seat squabs moved, you got this tremendous heat coming through!

The Series II was a successful car apart from quality. We had terrible problems with

quality but that was because of Leyland buying cheap components. They just didn't care about quality standards, they just wanted production. They produced far too many cars when the oil crisis came instead of flexing themselves.

It nearly killed Henlys and other dealers off. At that time we had a system Sir William had installed of direct debit. As soon as the car left the factory it was debited to the accounts of the distributors. BL/Jaguar management had increased the workforce enormously and kept producing with no market existing. The dealers had a meeting with our management and requested that not too many cars should be supplied to them because they were carrying too much stock, their banks were

screwing them and the position was very unsafe. They maintained that they were reassured. I don't know because I wasn't there.

I do know that by the time they went home that evening they thought all was fine. On the Monday morning their bank managers phoned them up and said, 'You know you've been debited £2m, £2½ m' or whatever it might have been. It almost bankrupted some of them. That's when all the trust went.

I was a Director for Leyland overseas and I was just told I was taking so many and I was just sent them whether I could sell them or not. The net result was that we had hundreds of cars, distressed stock, around the world. I was running the Belgium operation in '71 and I remember picking out hundreds of cars in Germany covered in rust and taking them back to Belgium and refurbishing them for British Leyland. The same thing happened again in '73 and '75. When we took over in 1983, we had 189 cars, old stock in Germany, same old story. It went on year after year. It was quite appalling.

The same Frankfurt show in 1973 saw the début of the delightfully stylish XJ coupés. A personal favourite of Sir

Indeed, enough was obviously thought of this creation to build such a front end, but surely this is too bland – and no Jaguar. (J.C.)

William's, they were perhaps the last really stylish true Lyons Jaguar.

Due to problems of sealing the pillarless side windows on their rubbers to maintain the low wind noise demanded, the XJ6Cs and XJ12Cs did not commence production until April 1975. The same month Jaguar, for reasons of economy, reintroduced the 3.4-litre engine into the range and achieved consumption figures in the order of 17-21 mpg. This engine, however, was rather different from the original 3.4, having a 4.2 type block and straight-port head. The 3.4 was not offered in the coupé version or in the States.

Also in April 1975 fuel injection was at last fitted to the V12 engines, first in the coupé and later in the saloons. This had the effect of increasing the power back to 285 bhp, allowed the engine to meet ever-stiffening pollution standards and improved consumption to 14 mpg.

Later in the year the XJ27, better known as the XJ-S, was introduced. It was no replacement for the venerable V12 E-type abandoned earlier in the year, but logically it was based on the shortened saloon platform and saloon suspension.

By this time the series of fuel crises had begun to beset the world and Jaguar production had to be cut as demand reduced. Hardly surprisingly the V12 engined cars were particularly hit.

As the XJ40 was obviously still some way off, Jaguar launched a Series III version of the evergreen XJ range in March 1979. It was intended to carry the company through to the new model and, once the quality problems were sorted out, this it did in no uncertain terms.

Due to styling commitments at Jaguar, Pininfarina was asked, in 1974, to put forward a proposal to improve the canopy treatment of the XJ body which appeared to be the area which was dating. Modifications to this proposal were made at Jaguar and this change became the Series III model. Approval for capital expenditure of £7m was not given till early 1976 due to the Ryder reorganisation of British Leyland. Drawings commenced in January 1976 with the intention of introduction in October 1978. The introduction had to be delayed until March 1979 for various reasons which will be explained in Chapter 3. This led to one of the most unfortunate new model introduction experiences in Jaguar history.

The windscreen was given greater rake, and a flatter roof line at the rear gave increased headroom for rear passengers. This flatter roof also allowed a metal sunshine roof to be offered. The screens were now glued in which made a better, leak-free, seal and increased shell rigidity. Various subtle changes modernised the car such as flush fitting door handles. Less subtle were the new black plastic bumpers which sprouted front and rear and, when sold in the States, incorporated the decreed 5 mph impact absorbing beams. Other new features included a cruise control, improved seating with electrical adjustment of height an option and an optional headlamp wash/wipe.

Sanity and the Jaguar grille return, and luckily good sense prevailed. (J.C.)

In September 1973 the Series II XJ6 and XJ12's were announced and many felt, and still do today, that the front end was improved by the facelift. So often Jaguar shapes have started pure and become diluted, but the XJ may be the exception. (J.C.)

In 1978 the Rover five-speed gearbox was adopted which meant the cessation of manufacture of the Jaguar four-speed and with it the option of a manual XJ-S.

As we shall see in the next chapter, concurrent with the production of the XJ variants. BL was wreaking havoc, and the infamous Ryder Report and its devotees at BL sought to submerge the identity of Jaguar. Many good people, whom Sir William had been grooming, gave up and resigned at the sheer frustration and incompetence. One former employee reckons most of the BL types he was forced to have meetings with were lucky if they could find their way home let alone manage a business. One of the loyal Jaguar men who fought longest and hardest to preserve the company's identity was Andrew Whyte, formerly in charge of PR and now writing, amongst others, excellent books on Jaguar.

As is now well known, quality was Jaguar's overiding problem of the seventies and very early eighties. The introduction of the Series III painted in the new Pressed Steel Fisher paint plant at Castle Bromwich added to the problems which were the subject of urgent action by the recently formed Quality Department. By the late seventies John Morgan was in Japan as Vice President of the BL company there.

Quality was dreadful. It cost us nearly £2000 a car to prepare them in order to sell them. We had no cars for six months after the Series III was launched.

'Suddenly they sent 750 cars over. Some

With the styling department busy on the XJ40, Pinin Farina was employed to produce an updated XJ Series III and this was his version with various refinements added by Jaguar. Note the split rear window with two slightly different treatments visible. (J.C.)

The pillarless XJ Coupé is surely the most stylish of all the XJ's and, for this reason plus the fact that relatively few were made, is destined to become a collectors' item. (P.H.P.)

came out with paint peeling off, on some the headlining was down on the seats and we had none of the colours or specifications we'd ordered. It took two and a half years to sort them all out.

Meanwhile I had come back to work for John Egan and was Sales Director for two and a half years. It was a dreadful time just disposing of old stocks, clearing the decks and trying to build up the image.

The whole range at the turn of the decade is seen here with Series III saloons standing beside examples of XJS, and spearheaded by the Daimler Limousine. (J.C.)

The Series IIIs were rather more radically revised with altered roofline and more subtle changes to maintain sales pending the arrival of the XJ40. (J.C.)

As the quality was gradually improved it was essential to convince the dealers, particularly in the US. So with the introduction of the HE V12 engine various cosmetic changes were made. The Daimler grille was dropped on the top model and it became a Jaguar Vanden Plas. More wood was adopted in the trim on other models in an attempt to distinguish them from previous cars.

I said to John that we had got to have the cars on the track so that they could see what they were going to be selling – so why not call them '82 models as we're almost there now. This was about March or April, 1981! So we dropped the '81, overdue as usual, and named the model the '82. These were real changes and we were able to show them our new range here with confidence. I remember J.L.E. looking out of his office one day, that July, at the marquee I had had erected in the front car park to show the dealers our 'new' 1982 range saying, 'I don't know, John, whether that's going to be your mausoleum or our salvation!'

It went very well. We persuaded the

Americans that we were building a better product, which we were, and that we had something on the track that was new and more attractive, and that we were really determined to go ahead. That did it. That turned the tide.

All the unions helped enormously. We took Warwick Castle for two nights and gave a candlelit party there. The Lord Lieutenant was marvellous and gave us the Shire Hall at Warwick for a cocktail party beforehand. The City of Coventry came and supplied flowers because the building here was so tatty. It was just wonderful. Everybody helped us. We'd no money, but we did it, and it worked.

The Jaguar Sovereign, née Daimler, was the car the next generation of designs had to succeed and exceed, and it is a measure of the car's excellence so many years on that the task was to prove no easy one. (J.C.)

Chapter 3
Project XJ40

The seventies were a period of turmoil and serious threat for Jaguar. At the beginning of the decade, the XJ6 was selling well with a two year order backlog but British Leyland began shooting itself in every part of its anatomy. As the once proud names of the British motor industry were drawn into the net the slow, painful destruction process began. Jaguar was no exception.

More than an era ended in 1972 when Sir William Lyons, due to British Leyland policy, had to retire at seventy from 'his' company. Bill Heynes had already taken well-earned retirement in 1969 and Wally Hassan followed in 1972. Lofty England succeeded Lyons, and Bob Knight had succeeded Heynes.

As the decade progressed, group politics bore more and more heavily upon Bob Knight. Project XJ40 – it was actually known as LC40 (Leyland Cars) by the bureaucracy of big brother – was to be a replacement, no easy task, for the XJ6. With Lyons gone, Knight, rightly famed for his pre-eminent engineering work, found himself in a new role as a reluctant stylist.

I once asked Lyons what was the basis on which he approached styling. He thought a long time and he couldn't really describe it. So eventually, under pressure, he said, 'Well, all I did, Knight, was try to do nice cars – no gimmicks, just nice cars'.

Lyons was a natural stylist who was responsible for the skin lines of all Jaguars until 1968 with the exception of the E-type. As such he understood intuitively the fundamentals of styling, of line and light since style is only perceived by virtue of reflected light. He had the most incredible flair for line. He was, probably, the best in the world. That would be my view.

He understood balance and proportion, which are the fundamentals of style. He hated lines that did not go anywhere. Lines running along a car had to be meaningful and either run the length of the car or, in the case of the canopy, be sympathetic to other lines that were running the length of the car.

I believe that a test for style is to walk slowly round a car at a distance of about five to ten yards, looking constantly at it, and to observe whether any light lines or reveal lines do any unexpected thing as you walk. If everything seems compatible, you have some sort of a possible job. If there are

sudden departures from the expected, like the tail end suddenly appears to jut out as you're walking past the front of the car, then you know you're in trouble. Unexpected cavities around the wheels are unacceptable.

I found that, to express a constructive opinion on a style, it was sometimes necessary to walk around the model and to look at it from different standpoints for anything up to an hour before venturing a balanced opinion.

Lyons would only pass off a body style when it was out in the open under a sky without a lot of reflections from buildings and that sort of thing. The last act in passing off a body style occurs with the viewing of the assembly of hardwood models which will be used for making the press tools. Lyons insisted that this hardwood 'model stack' should be finished in polished black, which is usually the hardest on the style.

In Lyons' opinion the toughest test for any car is to see it in very, very shiny black under a bright sky.

His ability to style cars depended on his rapport with a particular sheet metal worker and several wood workers who developed the style with him and who could

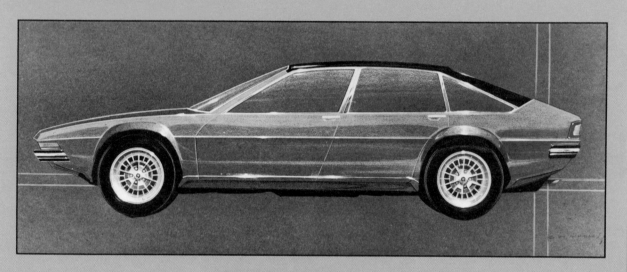

These various preliminary sketches, which are typical of those George Thompson actually started doing in 1971, were done in 1972 and were a little futuristic to say the least! (J.C.)

understand his requirements. Lyons could only appreciate a styling model in sheet metal, hence his dependence on one particular sheet metal worker.

When this one man left, Lyons had to try out about 20 others in order to find another with similar understanding. All styling sheet metal workers at Jaguar were, in fact, on contract from Abbey Panels because Lyons had run into trouble at some time in the past with the tinsmith's union. Eventually he found the right man and created the XJ6.

Lyons realised that styling would have to carry on after he left and a very small styling staff, with a studio, was formed starting in the late 1960s.

When Lyons ceased to take any interest in styling, which was not long before he left, it followed that there was this very small staff of styling artists and a woodwork shop containing one or two woodworkers and sheet metal workers, but none of them had any experience of developing full size models in clay which was the more generally used material.

The first attempts at a full size clay model of XJ40 started in about 1973 when two wooden bucks were made which were capable of accepting clay. The young Jaguar stylists were excellent artists with plenty of imagination and their drawings were highlighted to give the impression of the shape they wished to create. It then became apparent over the next two or three years that the highlights which could be achieved on the full size model were often not in accordance with their drawings. So the shape, therefore, looked different because everything depends on light reflections for the mental interpretation of shape.

There was, as a result, a long and weary learning curve. Full size clays, usually, departed from original intentions because, before they'd reached anywhere near finality, it became apparent that changes had to be made.

In the early stages, attempts were made at styles having a family resemblance and then there was pressure from outside Jaguar to produce something that was not at all like the existing car – completely fresh thinking. We gravitated all the way through

that into the final phase when everybody inside and outside Jaguar agreed that the style must continue the Jaguar tradition, in other words, look as if it was a lineal descendant.

Between 1969 and 1975 that outside influence coupled with the desire to smooth the thing, from the point of view of aerodynamic drag, did lead us through all sorts of very bland creations.

Tom Jones recalls that they would be visited by various British Leyland styling committees which would change their requirements each time they had a viewing.

There was no real money to get on with the job, even engineering-wise. Politics played a big part in the early days and there was a suggestion that we should use the Rover V8 engine instead of the new AJ6. There was a lot of pressure and Bob Knight fought that one off. The product planning crowd were Rover people and if we hadn't been careful at that time it would have been a reskinned Rover SD1. Anyway we fought that lot off and common sense prevailed in the end.

'I was determined not to have the Rover V8,' states Knight, who concedes that it is an excellent engine but a Jaguar needs a dedicated engine. 'It took a lot of arguing. A most intriguing thing happened later in that David Andrews and another BL Board member went over, in 1979, to General Motors and met various top men. One of them called Murphy said to them, 'if anybody got the idea of putting that engine into a Jaguar, they'd need their heads looking at'. I knew several GM men and it may be that I had a hand in that!'.

Initially most XJ40 work was confined to styling exercises as Styling battled with the unenviable task of trying to create a viable successor to the XJ6.

George Thompson had just completed his apprenticeship and, having spent the greater part of that period in the styling department, returned

there as a member of the small team headed by Doug Thorpe and also including Colin Holtum, the interior specialist who is still there, Oliver Winterbottom and Chris Greville-Smith. Knight was impressed by their work and Thorpe comments that Thompson, 'made a particulary good contribution'.

About 1971 I started picking up ideas, for XJ40, states Thompson. I was only 21 and was strongly influenced by what was going on at the time. They didn't really bear what I would consider now as a strong resemblance to Jaguars as they should have done. They were all exotica and looked like Lamborghinis! At the time we were looking to a launch in '77/78!

Initially we worked for Sir William, and still saw him after he relinquished control, and then Lofty England for a while, then Geoffrey Robinson and then Bob Knight – he used to hold my pencil! We used to have some great times, being there till three or four o'clock in the morning to get a model ready. Bob would be there, jacket off, out in the model shop making a tool to scrape the clay to get the right radius because he couldn't trust us to do it for him!

The first quarter scale model was done in October 1973 by Greville-Smith, Holtum and Knight. Colin Holtum remembers that, 'Mr England took that model, in the back of a Maxi, which was the only thing that was big enough to take it, down to London for a meeting with Stokes and Barber. It was used to say, 'Yes, we do need a replacement. Here's a car that supports the sort of ideas we're looking at'. Permission was given to progress and the model was then transferred into the full size'.

'And lost something on the way!' chipped in Geof Lawson, Chief Stylist today.

'This was viewed by the Board,' according to Thompson, 'but it had no character. It didn't flow the way Jaguars had done previously. That then led into a series of developments. I think that sometimes the stylists had

This is the first quarter-scale model to be made and the one which Lofty England took down to British Leyland for initial approval. (J.C.)

chairmanship. Robinson, with his strong Italian links, commissioned Guigiaro and Bertone to produce their thoughts for an XJ40. Cyril Crouch, Chief Body Engineer and another who played an important part in the XJ40 styling, was not impressed. 'None of them were much use – a lot of money was spent – but we didn't use any of them. We had a line-up of the various

one side of the model and Bob Knight had the other'.

Ironically one of the creations of this period had many of the features of the final car and yet, as we shall see, the path meanders considerably before returning once again. Holtum feels that this design was,

typical of the era, in '73, and would have made a good Series II. The XJS element was gradually being smoothed out to achieve a more saloon-looking front and different front end treatments were tried.

Then Pinin Farina bought an XJ12 off us in the Summer, drove down to Spain, spent his holiday there, then took the thing back and cut it to pieces and built his version which he put into a couple of motor shows. This came into the works as a thought provoker at the time and there was then an unsureness about whether the car we were doing was far enough advanced.

George Thompson did his own version.

I did a quarter-scale model using the same treatment of the wing line, disappearing into the door, the wrap-around on the bumper – everything fitting within the aperture on the front end including the grille and the lamps. Colin and I scaled straight up from the quarter scale and gave it to the modellers. When we put it outside, it looked very severe. I wasn't experienced enough in those days to realise that once you reach that first stage there was still a tremendous amount of work to do to refine

The similarity to the XJS is obvious but the distinctive headlamps and front wing treatment rather dictated the rest of the shape which Thompson feels is the wrong way to go about designing a car. (J.C.)

the shape of the vehicle – how much you can actually push and pull the lines, without changing the style but making tremendous improvements.

By this time Geoffrey Robinson, who had been at Innocenti making Minis, had arrived as MD, and soon after that Lofty England retired from the

Italian ones and a couple we'd done and Stokes came along and didn't think much of any of them, as I recall, apart from the Pininfarina one – an ugly looking brute in my opinion! He liked that best of all, much to the dismay of everyone else.'

Guigiaro actually turned up with two exercises. One was created for Jaguar and the other, it is assumed by various people I have spoken to, happened to be another exercise for a large saloon that he was working on. Colin states that, 'all it had was a large Jaguar badge'. George remembers that the

Approval was given and the first full size clay to be made at Jaguar was completed in February 1973, but in full size it looked rather less happy. (J.C.)

other one was known, at Browns Lane, as 'the gunship'! It is generally agreed, that the additional one ended up as the Maserati Quattroporte.

Colin Holtum expresses the feeling held by his colleagues. 'You stand as much chance of getting a good car out of the Italians as you do out of us, because they are experienced people, but what the company loses is the design history that created that car. What the Italians don't have is the Jaguar background. So we have found that, when we deal with outside people, they do a very professional product but they don't produce a Jaguar'.

As Bob Knight points out, the Italian styling houses evolve styles for manu-

A further variation on the same theme was then tried with one person taking one side and another the other side. (J.C.)

With Bob Knight's early thoughts on the left and George Thompson's on the right, two rather different motor cars are emerging. (J.C.)

By splitting and joining one normal and one reversed photograph these half body clays could be 'made' whole and viewed as such. (J.C.)

Top middle: By May 1973, a definite grille had appeared but the wing line was still raised in XJS style. (J.C.)

Right: This is the rear end treatment of the same May 1973 mock-up which Thompson recalls Lofty England having had some beneficial influence on. (J.C.)

Far right: By June 1973 we see a slight variation which is not too far removed from the final shape but a lot would happen before this thinking re-emerged. (J.C.)

Top right: A couple of months later and the wing line is now level with the bonnet but the grille is less 'Jaguar' though. As the Series II behind shows, however, this is more of an XJ with rectangular headlamps. (J.C.)

facturers all over the world. These styles tend to be similar regardless of the manufacturer for whom they are working.

Holtum states that, 'after the revue, the Italians were asked to go away and do some more work, and we also started looking at more revolutionary cars – this was the Origami period.

Looking back you think, why did we ever do anything like that, but it was all part of the process'.

Whilst all this was going on the politics were hotting up. British Leyland, unable to pay its purchase tax bill, had been nationalised in November 1974. Nobody knows more about this period, from Jaguar's point of view,

than Bob Knight who was well and truly in the thick of it.

'A feature of the proceedings as it was developing under the corporate set-up was a greater and greater involvement of central staffs and this was generating more and more paperwork. I remember making a check on this, in about '72, and around 25 per cent of my time was being taken by virtue of the fact that we were members of a large corporation'.

Top left: Meanwhile, quarter-scale models were still being done and this is one of George Thompson's which he says was inspired by a trip to the 1973 Geneva Show where he saw Guigiaro's design that became the Lotus Esprit. (J.C.)

This side view photographed in September 1973 shows another slight variation on the full size theme. Progress was definitely being made towards the eventual shape, but then a mixture of self-doubt and outside influences took a hand in matters. (J.C.)

This is Pininfarina's XJ12 seen at the factory in October 1973 and which made the Jaguar stylists wonder if they were being too conservative. (J.C.)

The side profile is, to me, pure Ferrari and looks quite stylish, though not a Jaguar. (J.C.)

The front end certainly is not a Jaguar and might be termed 'blunt'! (J.C.)

Top right: The Jaguar stylists, however, were influenced (and it is very easy for me to be critical in hindsight) by the Pinanfarina creation and came up with their own version. (J.C.)

Geoffrey Robinson, who had by now joined the company, commissioned a couple of Italian styling houses to submit their ideas for an XJ40 and this offering from Guigiaro was nicknamed at the factory, the 'gunship'. (J.C.)

Guigiaro also turned up with this extraordinary creation which he had put a Jaguar badge on. (J.C.)

Below: The Bertone rendering was less offensive but very plain, over-heavy in style and certainly no Jaguar. (J.C.)

The Italian influence was clearly getting to the Jaguar stylists who produced this one to line up alongside the Latin offerings in June 1974. It reminds Geof Lawson of a Toyota Corolla! (J.C.)

Sir Don Ryder was commissioned by Anthony Wedgwood Benn to report on possible reorganisation of British Leyland. His committee included a number of Ford men. The resulting 'Ryder Report' caused, in Knight's words, 'stark dismay at Jaguar' when published in the Spring of 1975. It is relatively well-known in Jaguar circles that Bob Knight saved the Engineering Department from the worst of their recommendations. Indeed Jim Randle, his successor as Engineering Director, stated to me recently that the alternative, 'would have meant annihilation of the product. Under the guidance of Bob Knight, we spent enormous

amounts of time working out the politics of keeping us free. That was a pretty unhappy time. Every week we had to work out the next bit of strategy and I think immense credit goes to Bob that through his efforts we did stay free, because had Jaguar Engineering got sucked in, then the company could not have stood on its own'.

A number of senior managers I spoke to feel similarly strongly reckoning that credit for the very survival of Jaguar is due to Knight.

So how did Bob achieve this vital success over the advocates of total centralisation?

This is what Colin Holtum describes as the 'Origami' period of flat surfaces and sharp folds. All pretence to be a Jaguar has gone and the pressure to be more revolutionary was being felt. (J.C.)

The stylists themselves wonder now how they could have produced these, but it was all part of the learning curve and one has to remember that it was more than ten years ago, in fact, August 1974 to be precise. (J.C.)

Organisation on individual company lines ceased to exist in that the functions within these companies were to be controlled by a central staff. Below central director level even more chopping up was proposed. For example, engineering such as power unit, body, chassis and electrical design was to be controlled not by a company engineering director but by various supremos located in different parts of the corporation.

Fortunately, we persuaded Ryder that that wasn't good for Jaguar Engineering and it was the only part of the Ryder Report not to be implemented.

The non-Jaguar school continued into 1975 and this is one result seen in March of that year. (J.C.)

By September 1975 the shape had softened a little and a few curves had re-entered the equation; for anything other than a Jaguar this might have been perceived to be a stylish car of the period. (J.C.)

Of the situation elsewhere in the corporation Charles Griffin of Austin Morris said to me, 'There is no doubt, Bob, we have achieved a new way of making the engineering of cars even more difficult'.

[But how, I pressed Bob, did he actually retain Jaguar Engineering integrity?]

I used to fight with cars. During the very early Spring, 1975, when the Ryder committee was deliberating, Ryder had a burn out in his Rolls-Royce and needed a new car. He thought he'd better have a Jaguar, so he ordered a 4.2 This car was, therefore, prepared for him. In the meantime, we had done the fuel injected version of the XJ12 which was clearly a very good car, especially by the standards of the day.

So I got a pre-production one and prepared that for Ryder as well. When the

time came for the chauffeur to collect the car from the then office block on the Marylebone Road in London, we sent the XJ12 down. The chauffeur refused to take delivery. He said his instructions were to take delivery of the 4.2. Eventually the chauffeur was persuaded to take the car, at least for the purposes of the long journey that Ryder had to make next day.

After that, there was a day of complete silence. On the following day at 9 o'clock in the morning, Ryder rang Geoffrey Robinson and purred into the telephone about this incredible motor car. He said we could forget the 4.2, he wanted the V12; which is exactly what I'd wanted, of course.

So Ryder was weaned on to the XJ12

Around 1974/75 an American called Roger Zrimec joined the Jaguar styling department and was to exert considerable influence for a while looking for more revolutionary answers. (J.C.)

and was tremendously impressed by it. It was really this experience which caused Ryder to keep Jaguar Engineering as an entity.

The rest of the business did not escape

On these models dating back to December 1975, Zrimec had the left-hand side and Thompson, who feels that the Fiat 130 influenced him, worked on the right. (J.C.)

saddled with the job of Managing Director of this strange Leyland Cars organisation, and said, 'How about it? We need something at Jaguar to restore morale damaged by the absence of a Jaguar Board. What can you do?'

This resulted in Whitaker offering an Operating Committee with some central personnel and several Jaguar people, which made it a bit like a Board.

and the Jaguar Board was disbanded. Robinson departed and eventually entered politics. Opinions about him at Jaguar vary. Some feel he paid too much heed to the factory unions.

Bob Knight recounts the next chapter in the drama:

Between 1969 and 1974, Jaguar had contributed £24m positive cash flow which in the money of those times was a lot. That was, in effect, bullion that was hauled over the gate at Browns Lane and poured down the bottomless pit at Longbridge. This money could have made all the difference to Jaguar because it could have been used to provide Jaguar with a new body assembly shop and paint shop, and would have allowed us to pay decent salaries to attract, and keep, engineers. Jaguar would have been transformed by '74.

I tried to go further than just the Engineering Department with Ryder. I felt I must make an attempt to improve things as far as the factories were concerned. So I saw Derek Whitaker, who had been

Returning to the subject of styling, in
1974 an American called Roger Zrimec
joined Jaguar from Chrysler. Bob
Knight comments that he did some 'free
thinking, sensible styles' and Colin
Holtum feels that although many of his
ideas were rather too revolutionary for
Jaguar, he certainly influenced the
trend for a while. A number of the clays
were split with Zrimec working on one
side and other members of the department taking the opposite side.

In May 1976 Bertone and Guigiario
presented their second offerings. Bob
Knight puts his view succinctly. 'They
got worse!'

*'There was nothing spared trying to
generate ideas for the car. The Bertone
offering was probably the most tolerable of
the lot. Some of our styles were rather
bland but blandness is often the product of*

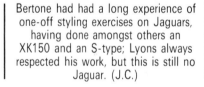

*clean lines. You just can't have bold
features that lend character, like the four
headlamp treatment on the original XJ6. If
you smooth things out, you're bound to
lose character.*

Bob Blake, the American foreman of
the Jaguar Styling Shop, was a brilliant
artist in sheet metal. He joined the
company from Cunningham in the
fifties after he had made all Cunningham's racing bodies. Jaguar first
met him at Le Mans and he assisted
with the creation of many of the Jaguar
models including the XJ40 before his
retirement.

We looked at face-lifts on the original XJ and I did a lot of experimentation with clay to see what we could do. Bob Knight had some good ideas but some might say they were 'fuddy duddy'. But he was 'fuddy duddy' with reason, 'cause nothing Bob Knight did, wasn't well thought out. He was very methodical and he never forgot what had been done and when it had been done. I always thought, though, that Bob was not quite adventurous enough.

I and the other boys in styling would try to present a rather more radical line hoping he would come some way towards it and he would a little bit. That little space between his ears is better than a computer. Anything that's gone in can be repeated almost verbatim at any time thereafter – he's an IBM on feet! Consequently he was able to say on such and such a date we tried that and I didn't like it. That's the way an engineer works, which is why he is so damn good as an engineer, but it's not the way a stylist works.

Talking of corporate interference Doug Thorpe reckons. 'I've lost count of the number of styling reviews there were. It was only when the corporate influence evaporated that we reached any real decision. I remember being rebuked by Lord Stokes who said to me once, 'The only Jaguar thing I want to see on this car next time I come back is the badge on the front'.

Cyril Crouch, remembering that at one stage British Leyland wanted something akin to a one and a half times full size Allegro, expresses a feeling mentioned to me by many.

During that period we had so many changes in the management and each time we had a different man at the top the requirements changed! Bob and I spent an enormous amount of time in the styling shop working with the people on the clay to get this thing into something like a Jaguar shape, whilst the expensive Italian efforts were put under wraps and collected dust. Occasionally Bob would say let's have a look at that thing of Bertone's to see how something was done, but we'd still do our own thing.

These were trying times for Jaguar's beleagured management and the BL people felt that the XJ6 was old fashioned and must be made more Germanic. (J.C.)

We wanted to improve the interior width and improve the aerodynamics without increasing the overall width. We always wanted to see as much as possible of the front of the car from the driving seat, a strong feature of the XJ6. Another essential was to retain the Jaguar grille.

Knight agrees and expands the point. 'We always felt that the owner of an expensive car likes to see an expanse of a bonnet in front of him. The XJ6 was particularly good in this respect and one could see, from the driving seat, to within a few centimetres of the actual front of the car. The wing crown line was an excellent feature which we wished to retain, though it caused some difficulty to do so'.

Cyril Crouch: 'Obviously we had to keep it a Jaguar, rather than the way-out things visualised by the BL

Still the blandness continued in August 1976 and the Jaguar grille seemed lost forever! (J.C.)

Board. Bob Knight was quite a forceful character in that respect and resisted the attempts to bring in other stylists from within the group'.

Colin Holtum feels that the Jaguar influence started to reassert itself again in the styling around 1976, although he points out the Fiat 130 influence in 1977 also reminiscent of the Ferrari 400. 'The dominance of the grille started to come back again and by 1978 the final shape was starting to emerge'.

Bob Knight takes up the story again.

Apart from trying like hell to find something to follow the XJ6 in style, one obviously had to be concerned with fuel consump-

By December 1976 the lines were beginning to soften and, is that the signs of a grille reappearing? (J.C.)

By March 1977 the answer is yes, as a definite grille reappears, though the general shape is still very boxy. (J.C.)

tion. If you reduce weight by 10 per cent, you reduce the accelerative forces required by 10 per cent and you reduce the rolling resistance by 10 per cent. Reducing the drag by 10 per cent, obviously reduces the aerodynamic forces by 10 per cent. If you then reduce the engine swept volume by 10 per cent, you get a 10 per cent improvement in fuel economy.

We ran cars, for other purposes, unladen and fully laden for quite long distances – like 15,000 miles – and one result I remember was that for a 17 per cent reduction in weight, with nothing else done, there was only a 5 per cent reduction in fuel consumption. Thus all other requirements have to be reduced in proportion in order to achieve a worthwhile change.

From that point onwards it is the specific consumption characteristics of the power unit which matter. So we decided to go ahead with a new six-cylinder power unit (covered in detail in Chapter 5) which was not only going to be lighter, by a considerable margin, but also was going to be better for specific consumptions. It was designed to accept two types of cylinder head – the Michael May high compression head which was under development for the twelve-cylinder engine and the four-valve head.

We used the MIRA wind tunnel to compare the full size clay to a standard

XJ6. *With the underside of both so treated that they were comparable, the tests indicated that the drag coefficient of the XJ40 would be .35 compared to .43/.44 for the Series III.*

As far as side window treatment was concerned, we put flushing panels along the side, so that in effect we had a smooth side, but there was hardly any perceptible change in drag!

The importance of refinement, ride and handling was uppermost in my mind, but ride and refinement especially, because I'd striven so hard from 1954 to achieve higher and better standards.

In April, 1978 the first detailed weight estimate was compiled. This was based on the early schemes of the vehicle and forecast a weight of 3350 lb with power-assisted steering, air conditioning and power unit. Efforts to reduce weight led Knight to compare MacPherson strut systems with the double wishbone set-up. But he found that, 'they can be surprisingly similar in weight'.

The problem is always to find room for suspension assemblies. For that reason my views were that the front body side members should be at about the same height as front bumpers designed to meet American legislation; partly to get control of the crush conditions for barrier impact test purposes and partly because a lot more space was created for the front suspension.

Increasing space frees up the design and helps in decreasing weight.

Regarding rear suspension, many manufacturers employ semi-trailing wishbones usually mounted on a vee-shaped transverse member. At the point of the vee is the final drive unit and the ends of the vee are mounted elastically to the body sills, which is a good thing. We stubbed our toes in the middle sixties on a suspension with a short torque tube having a mounting at the middle of the heel board crossmember. This transmitted a significant amount of noise and vibration. The drawback of this semi-trailing arrangement is one of space, and the problem is the accommodation of the exhuast system. By and large cars that have this system can't have silencers under the rear seats, which is an advantage of the Jaguar layout. I have always disliked the semi-trailing wishbone for the reasons of the limitations of space, which partly arose because the XJ6, and therefore inevitably its successors, is low. The remarkable thing about the XJ6 when it appeared was its lowness which, incidently, put months on the design and engineering time.

Jaguar's independent rear suspension has always been highly regarded by commentators but perfectionist Bob Knight outlines areas that he felt could be improved upon.

'There were three snags with the Jaguar suspension. First of all, the inclusion of the dampers within the suspension assembly, which assembly was then rubber mounted to the body, resulted in more motion being imparted to the suspension assembly mass than was desirable. It did no harm, but it meant that there was at least one mode of vibration from road input which you'd rather not have.

'I proved this point in 1964 with an S-type saloon by putting dampers direct to the body. There was an observable improvement in secondary ride. So we'd always wanted to move the dampers from within the suspension assembly'.

Knight also discovered what he calls a trailing link effect.

In the early 1960s I was driving an E-type at high speed on the M45 and had reason to open and shut the throttle over some rather wavy pieces of road. I then realised that with the throttle open the pitch frequency of the car was lower. With the throttle shut, it rose. I soon realised that the trouble lay in the trailing links. When you have the throttle open, particularly in the

> Meanwhile, 40 mph frontal impact testing was being carried out on XJs and although the greater speed resulted in a dramatic appearance, the windscreen remained in tact. (BL)

low gears, you have a lot of compression on the links. This results in a reduction of the effective rear spring rate. In some makes of car, employing trailing links, this effect is very obvious.

The third matter mentioned by Knight is inboard-mounted brakes, as on the Jaguars, as opposed to outboard.

Strangely enough the concept that unsprung weight should be held to an absolute minimum is not necessarily right.

It's quite good from the point of view of adhesion. From the point of view of secondary ride, it frequently isn't the case because it depends on the relationship between wheel bounce resonant frequency and other resonances in the vehicle which can be excited by that.

Sometimes, and particularly at the front end, it pays to have a lower wheel bounce frequency and greater unsprung weight in order to get the wheel balance resonant frequency away from the pitch resonance of the power unit on its mountings.

It was, therefore, decided to go to outboard brakes because that simplified mounting of the diff unit and eliminated the transmission of heat from the brake discs into the final drive unit.

There were various design attempts on this before I retired but it seems there has since been considerable progress developing the concepts into a proper sophisticated job containing those three elements of change.

Above: This view of the floor, tunnel and dash of the front passenger compartment after the first 40 mph test shows that there is work to be done but the engine has not broken through. (BL)

With these tests Jaguar were able to launch an eventual replacement that built on the XJs inherently strong construction and was ahead of any anticipated legislation. As can be seen here, however, this one may be a low mileage car but is now decidedly secondhand! (BL)

Returning to the political situation, the Ryder inspired Leyland Cars organisation came to its end in November 1977. Michael Edwardes, a member of the National Enterprise Board, was appointed to carry out yet another reorganisation of the corporation which was now to be called BL Limited. He hinted that decentralisation was to be a feature of the change. Knight was grateful for such thinking because of the time consumed responding to central staffs who inevitably wished to justify their positions.

Edwardes had considerable faith in psychological tests for senior management. Knight was supposed to attend to be tested in the very first wave.

But I didn't as I wanted to find out what was going on! Presumably I did fairly well because, when I was interviewed afterwards by Edwardes, he didn't bother with the results but asked me what I thought of the psychologist!

He was proposing a 'Jaguar Rover Triumph' organisation and sketched out the structure saying, 'I wonder what you would feel about taking control of JRT engi-

Returning to the styling, during the early months of 1977 a prodigious number of slight variations on the same theme were sculpted and by July the grille was certainly in favour even if the body was still a little anaemic. (J.C.)

neering as a whole?' That, of course, sent a fair old chill down my spine because it was obvious to me that the JRT structure depicted could easily become a smaller version of Leyland Cars.

I said that I felt that he would want me to give some responsible thought as to how I could operate his proposal before giving my reply. I said I would like the opportunity to give my comments on his proposed JRT structure. Edwardes agreed I could do this provided that I could present my views within four days on not more than four pages.

I put forward my sincerely felt arguments in favour of separate company organisations reporting to a Jaguar Rover Triumph administrator which he appeared to want. This apparently carried the day and it was decided there would be managing directors for the three companies. Almost inevitably I was one of them.

William Pratt Thompson, an American,

was appointed Chairman of JRT but there were still battles to be fought and the 'centralisers' tried to make the most of the JRT structure. After a good deal of argument it was decided that Sales and Marketing, Finance, Product Planning and Purchase would be JRT functions. This was a disappointment to Knight but at least he had control of

My slight sarcasm should not be taken as criticism of the stylists who, in the difficult circumstances of the period, did a fine job and have the confidence to admit today that they were learning. (J.C.)

Manufacturing and Engineering and could recreate a Jaguar Service Department. In order to improve action on quality problems, he appointed the now very experienced and energetic, David Fielden as Quality Director and Neville Neal as Service Director.

What stylist in the world would envy the Jaguar men, who had to follow in the footsteps of 'the master', Sir William Lyons, who began visiting the department again with increasing frequency and made an invaluable contribution towards the detail work. (J.C.)

Interestingly Bob Knight always felt that, for his money a Jaguar owner should have a sight of the full extent of his car's bonnet from the driving seat. (J.C.)

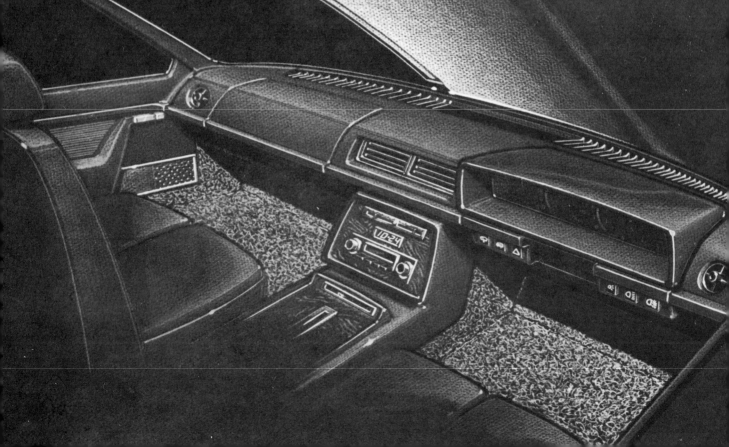

Left insert: It is March, 1978 and the Jaguar elements are returning with, apart from the grille, the familiar profile to the bonnet. (J.C.)

Right: For a while is seemed certain that a Jaguar was going to be plastic like almost all other cars. This would have left most traditional owners speechless if not bereft of life! (J.C.)

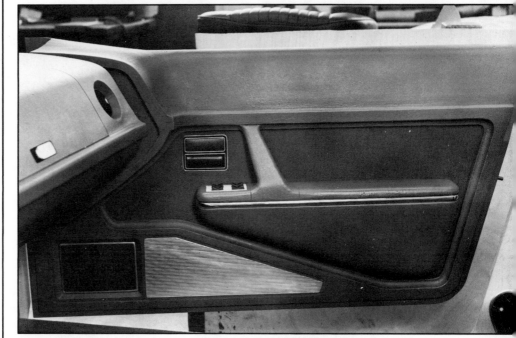

Left: The same car from the front three-quarter angle is looking more stylish but still a little angular with no sign as yet of the subtle Jaguar 'hip' that I feel makes so much difference. (J.C.)

Right: Considerations of cost and production over style and distinction nearly made the Jaguar craftsmen redundant in an age of growing uniformity. (J.C.)

Left: This is an early interior proposal when tradition was thought to be bunk. (J.C.)

Right: The Americans said 'no', and proved that not everything has to be tasteless to be modern. (J.C.)

The Service and Quality functions were complimentary because it was necessary to get proper service complaints information from the field together with failed components upon which the Quality Director could act.

Most of the quality problems emanated from suppliers and particularly the BL body assembly and paint plant at Castle Bromwich which was responsible for painting the new Series III bodies. As Knight recalls:

In the 12 months, following the introduction of Series III in March, 1980, we only got 40 per cent of the production we needed due to Castle Bromwich problems. In the end we were so desperate, we would take anything that was roughly the right shape, even if it was different colours either end!

All of the track motors in the paint shop were changed three times to overcome breakdowns. There was constant banditry on the 'drill deck', the area where holes were put into bodies to meet different markets specifications. Most importantly there was no hospital facility for paint rectification and such work had to be carried out in the condemned paint shop at Browns Lane.

We managed to arrange for a BL audit to be done on quality and I would get daily telexes which would read, for example, as follows; 'bodies off shift – 28, bodies acceptable – nil, bodies accepted by Jaguar – 28'. We lost £35m that year but there was nothing we could do but accept anything that was roughly the right shape. Gradually we brought about changes that enabled us to get proper control.

The worst suppliers were the big companies manufacturing major proprietary equipment. The ultimate weapon is the threat to change supplier, but it can take two or three years to approve and procure a major component such as a final drive unit or a transmission from another supplier. We had had serious problems with window lift switches on the earlier XJ6's. On the Series III we used a simplified and plain circuitry – previously the front seat ones overode the rear – so that we could use simpler switches and a switch for which there was

a direct Hella replacement. You can't do that with an axle or transmission.

There were yet further organisational changes in 1979 when Pratt Thompson was transferred to Leyland International. Land Rover became a separate entity within the corporation being removed from JRT. Percy Plant had been, involved in several winding up operations within the corporation. Senior Jaguar and Rover Triumph personnel hoped that his appointment as Chairman of JRT would mean the eventual demise of that organisation. Further devolution appeared to be intended and Product Planning became a company responsibility. Later Company Finance Directors were appointed but curiously the Purchase Department was handed to Rover Triumph.

During this period, in respect of Jaguar engineering, Jim Randle was appointed Director of Vehicle Engineering, and Harry Mundy, Director – Power Units and Transmissions.

Meanwhile it was essential that progress continued to be made with the XJ40 in spite of all the turmoil and uncertainty, and by now, of course, lack of capital in the group for investment in Jaguar. Knight continued to take an interest in the unenviable task of trying to create a shape to follow the Series III. 'I did take a considerable hand in it myself in the styling shop, often unwelcome, but I was merely trying to put in my two penn'orth to try to get some progress and to try to ensure that whatever happened wasn't too totally dissimilar to what had gone before'.

The development of the XJ40 style along more traditional Jaguar lines was bearing fruit. Bob Knight again:

It had been agreed about 1977 that there should be some sort of family resemblance and by February 1980 we'd got something that was not too bad. I had hoped to develop this a little further but to my surprise the style was accepted as it stood with the qualification that certain details of the bonnet and screen wiper treatment could be improved.

The Jaguar elements that had been returning to the exterior shape since the late seventies were now joined by a further softening, a distinctive 'Jaguar' grille and the XJ 'hip'. Left: The rear end is nearly there but the boot lid lacks the slight 'spoiler' lip of the final car. Top: The side view of this near-final mock-up shows that we have turned full circle and returned to Sir William's original XJ theme. (J.C.)

As far as I can see this is the style that has gone into production. The clay was sent at that point to Pressed Steel Fisher for detail measurement and for what is known as 'computer smoothing'. Over the next three months a 'see-through' model was made in fibre-glass from the clay.

In March, 1980 I was informed that the Castle Bromwich body assembly and paint plant was to become part of the Jaguar organisation.

Harry Mundy retired due to ill health in March 1980 and Knight appointed Trevor Crisp in his place. Jim Randle was then appointed overall Engineering Director.

Bob Knight, the loyal and brilliant Jaguar man, retired in July 1980, concentrating subsequently on consultancy work to the considerable benefit of his eminent clients. He states that he is still not very happy with the XJ40 shape, but in this, – and I have told him, so – I think he is wrong.

The fibre-glass 'see-though' model was to be used for external styling clinics. A document produced by Jim Randle, for BL in January 1981 states under the heading of 'Body Exterior Style', the following: 'To confirm the acceptability of the style, two clinics were held at Effingham Park and Harrogate in June 1980 . . . The results were extremely favourable, the model scoring the highest points ever achieved at a British Leyland clinic on any car of either our own or of competitor's manufacture'.

It is questionable whether Bob Knight's role, both in terms of engineering brilliance and fighting to save the identity and future of Jaguar, has ever been fully recognised and adequately acknowledged. (J.C.)

Chapter 4
Approval to Reality

'I guess if I'd known the size of the task I'd have chickened out. I was blissfully ignorant in 1980!' So Jim Randle, who had assumed responsibility for the XJ40 upon Knight's retirement and was to mastermind the whole project, modestly states.

George Mason, 27 years at Jaguar and Supervisor of the Experimental Workshops, expresses it rather more bluntly. 'It's been a ball-breaker, to put it mildly. I maintain it's taken a few years out of all our lives, it's been one hell of a challenge but it's worked out in the end.'

John Egan had joined the company in April 1980 as full-time Chairman and took over Bob Knight's crusade. 'Egan galvanised the place,' states Doug Thorpe. 'You could see who was on the bridge – one person there and not about fifteen.'

When he arrived, the company was on strike. Jim Randle remembers it well. 'It seemed quite certain we were going to close. I had all of the machines covered over and got the people together and said, 'Well, it's

been a good time chaps. I've enjoyed working with you. I don't really expect to see you again. Cheerio.'

John Egan spent his first Saturday and Sunday with the company discussing the situation with the union representatives and management. He managed to persuade them of his commitment to the company and his

determination to succeed. By a small majority vote the strike was ended and production resumed.

In September 1980, the XJ40 proto-

The first prototype XJ40 emerges from the Experimental shop in July 1981. Jim Randle can be seen second from the right. (J. Randle)

The moment of reckoning as Jim Randle drives the prototype away on its maiden journey with the absence of trim showing what a difference that can make to a style. (J. Randle)

Randle and colleagues head out of the factory off to Gaydon to complete the first of the 5,500,000 miles that development cars were to cover. (J. Randle)

This test vehicle, actually an XJ6 being driven by Norman Dewis, gives some idea of the interior of a development car. (J.C.)

type schedules were issued and although it was intended that the first SEP (semi-engineered prototype) would be completed by early 1981, it was not in commission until 15 July. George Mason remembers it well. 'Jim Randle, plus about another dozen of us, took it across to Gaydon that night and although it was only something like one third trimmed and we'd got a few bangs and bumps where things were hitting where they shouldn't be hitting. I think we were all of the opinion we'd got ourselves a bloody good motor car trying to get out from underneath us! We were all reasonably excited about it. The problem then was that we were committed to build at a rate and it was difficult to build at this rate with a lack of parts. When we started testing, things didn't go 100 per cent right, to put it mildly.'

In fact, as Norman Dewis recalls, testing had already begun before this. 'Because of the hold-up on producing the first body, we were involved doing a lot of the development work on the engine, suspension and gearbox using an XJ6. The theoretical weight of the XJ40 had been calculated, because the feeling was that all our previous models had been on the heavy side, and an XJ6 was modified to simulate the XJ40 in weight.

'We did that by taking out all the seats, the trim, that sort of thing and, I believe, we even took the doors off. Various suspensions were tried and we constructed some bodywork to simulate the drag coefficients of the '40'. It was mainly used to look at fuel consumptions and performance values of the 2.9 and 3.6 engines.'

Following the simulators, five SEPs were built. SEP 1 was a four-valve 3.6 manual and SEP 2 a two-valve 3.6 auto for use on road load data and structural testing. The next one, completed in early 1982, was used for ride and handling and was also a 3.6 auto but with the four-valve head. SEPs 4 and 5 were both manual 2.9's with two-valve heads and were used, respectively, for brake and electrical work.

There then followed twenty FEPs (fully-engineered prototypes) beginning with FEP 1 completed on 20 September 1982 and culminating numerically with FEP 20 finished in August 1983, though numbers 18 and 19 were not actually built until June and October, respectively, the following year. Not all were complete cars. For example, FEP 5 was used for 'methods built appraisal by Manufacturing' and FEP 8 was merely a body-in-white (unpainted bare bodyshell) used for safety tests. Ten of the FEPs were fitted with 3.6 engines, all four-valve, and the remaining six built had 2.9 power units. No less than twelve of the sixteen completed were fitted with automatic transmission.

As mentioned, one of the major areas

development status (the White Book), stated, 'The weight identified in the Programme Submission is 1510 Kg including a ZF transmission, 31 Kg above target'. The accompanying illustration taken from the report shows the state of play at that time.

Quite obviously low weight can be a virtue when trying to build a sporting, but above all – and remember how sensitive the issue was at that time – an economical car. But equally a Jaguar is a Jaguar because of its superb, arguably unparalleled, refinement. 'Lightweight panels,'' explains Jones, 'are

> Jaguars are justly famous for their refinement but refinement equals weight as the engineers discovered. (J.C.)

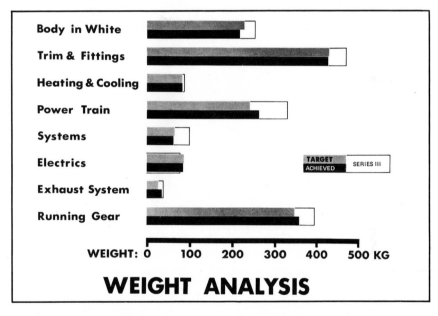

WEIGHT ANALYSIS

where the aim was to improve over the Series III was in weight. This, however, was to prove far more difficult than at first envisaged. As the engineers were to discover it is a truism that weight equals refinement and vice versa. Tom Jones comments, tongue in cheek, that 'if you don't break anything, you've over-engineered it'!

In January, 1981 a report compiled for the BL Board by Engineering to indicate the then present design and

more receptive to noise. Also the spec was increased during the project with things like electric rise and fall of the seat – it's all adding weight.'

On the same topic, George Mason adds:

We started off with parts on the light side and things start to break, and then you start a stepping-up operation. It's a new way of doing things for Jaguar. In the past we always engineered 'belt and braces', conse-

quently we had a very heavy car but a heavy car could be made very refined. But trying to refine a light car is another problem.

The rear and front suspension gave problems in the early days. The components were too light and would break. We were having to produce cars at such a volume and also test cars. We are not like Production who make a car and then it's sold. In here, you make a car, then you test it and so you are obliged to support it. Then you find you are being drained of all your labour resources all over the place and, of course, it meant a lot of midnight oil, and I mean a lot of midnight oil.

Digressing somewhat a moment, a lack of weight is not always necessarily seen as a virtue. Richard Cresswell recalls, with amusement, one experience he had whilst based in the States. 'I was astounded to hear an American salesman telling potential Jaguar customers that 'this car weighs two tons, you know' and what a good thing that was. That told an American that it was a comfortable riding car. I was horrified when I heard him. It was the very opposite of what we were striving for so hard!'

Moving on to the body construction, I talked to Cyril Crouch.

Having finalised the shape, we had to stitch it together with the construction inside it. This was my normal engineering job along with the engineers that I had. As we had done historically, we would prepare basic schemes for the interior structure and pass this on to Pressed Steel Fisher and they would do the product draft. We hadn't got the staff or facilities to do a complete engineering package down to final detail.

We did all the development for the front end, for instance, on the crushability of the front members, and employed PSF more or less as a contract office to churn out the production drawings from the schemes prepared by my people.

At the time we discussed what power unit we were going to put in the XJ40 because this influenced the positioning of

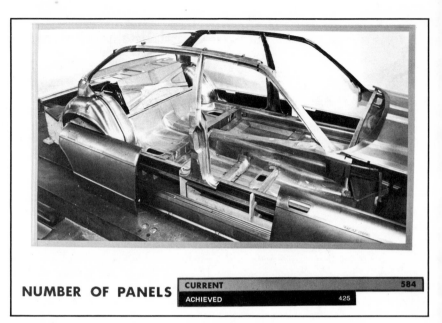

NUMBER OF PANELS CURRENT 584 ACHIEVED 425

A body/chassis construction similar to the earlier XJs was employed but more sophisticated tooling reduced the number of panels considerably. (J.C.)

the crushable members. 'Are we going to use the 5.3?' 'Oh, no' it was decided. The AJ6 was going to do everything the 5.3 did in performance and economy, and it was going to be a tremendous weight saver. So off we embarked on the front end structure ignoring the V12 on the assurance that the six-cylinder was going to do everything required of it!

As is now relatively well known, this turned out to be an unfortunate decision with the benefit of hindsight. Rather later in the programme it was learnt that, contrary to what one would imagine in this fuel conscious day and age, arch rivals BMW and Mercedes-Benz were building V12 engines. A U-turn was decreed and extensive re-engineering dictated later.

'We thought,' explains Tom Jones, 'that legislation was coming that required a 40 mph crash barrier test.' In fact work on this had commenced in the early seventies and a document entitled 'Interim Report on Computer Simulation to Assess 40 mph Frontal Impact of XJ12/40' had been issued on

15 March 1973. This book is not large enough to give in full the name of the British Leyland Department that produced it!

Taking odd sentences from this we learn that, 'The energy absorption capacity of the present XJ12 fender/valance structure is inadequate to meet the requirements of a 40 mph barrier test. Fortunately the stiffness of the Mk 1 (Series I) dash structure is sufficient to stop the vehicle before catastrophic engine intrusion.'

Tom Jones again: 'What it meant was that the subframe we mount the front suspension on had to be changed. So instead of the legs going forward, they went rearwards. Going from a 30 mph impact to 40 mph is equivalent to 40 squared over 30 squared, which is the same as 16 over 9, so it has a ratio of 16 to 9, thus there is nearly twice the energy to be absorbed.'

The bodyshell is of conventional integral design with a braced floorpan stiffened by large sill sections. The front crush tubes are attached to the prop shaft tunnel and sills, ensuring that in the event of a severe frontal impact, the crash forces are diverted round or under the passenger compartment.

Once the outer body skin had been

These futuristic sketches, typical of many done by George Thompson in the early seventies, and the first full-size model of the definitive XJ40 shape of 1980, shows clearly how styling of the final car came full circle. (J.C.)

Considerable testing was done from
the Jaguar base in Phoenix, Arizona
and by mid-May 1986 a million miles
had been clocked up here. (J.C.)

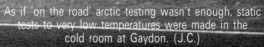

Canada provides conditions similar in their harshness to those of Arizona, but opposite in character, with temperatures down to –40°C. This shot gives an example of how simple camouflage can transform the appearance of a car. (J.C.)

As if 'on the road' arctic testing wasn't enough, static tests to very low temperatures were made in the cold room at Gaydon. (J.C.)

The 'buggy', used to subject components to the rigorous régime of the pavé, has now covered the equivalent of nearly 800,000 normal road miles and looks fit for at least the same again. (J.C.)

Sensibly Jaguar give style greater priority than low drag although some attention has been paid to 'cleaning up' the shape. Here an XJ40 is being given the wool-tuft treatment which gives a visual indication of airflow.

This rig, built by Cirrus, was for testing the Jaguar Diagnostic System which will make fault finding more of a science than an art. (J.C.)

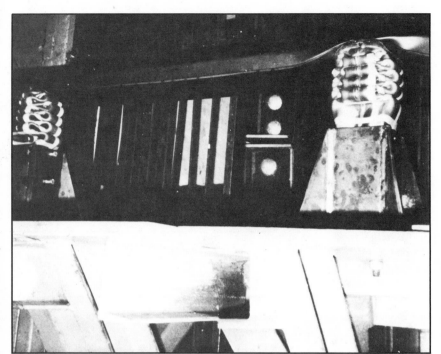

Optimum crash performance is obtained by achieving a progressive crush with the graph climbing steeply at the commencement as the area in front of the engine gives to absorb the inital impact. (J.C.)

finalised, the entire external surface was 'digitised', that is, gauged and recorded digitally by a computer. From this information drawings, and tooling could be accurately prepared. An important improvement over the car's forerunners was in the number of panels employed. The XJ40 has 25 per cent, namely 136, fewer pressings which not only means a stronger shell with fewer seams and joints, but it is also faster to build and more consistently accurate. The side structure used to

To improve the crush characteristics of the body, the XJ40 incorporates convoluted crush tubes. (J.C.)

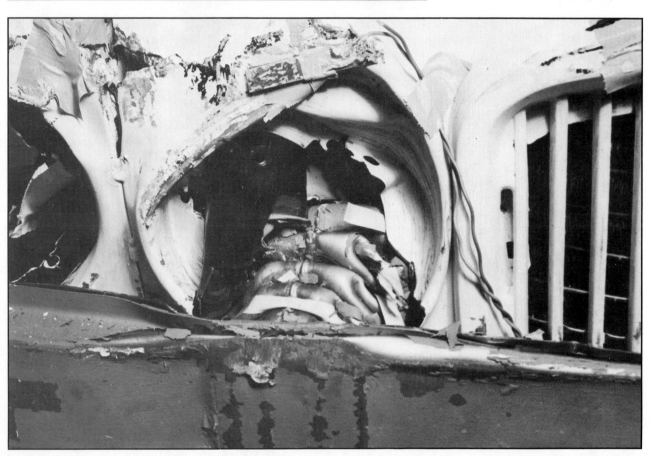

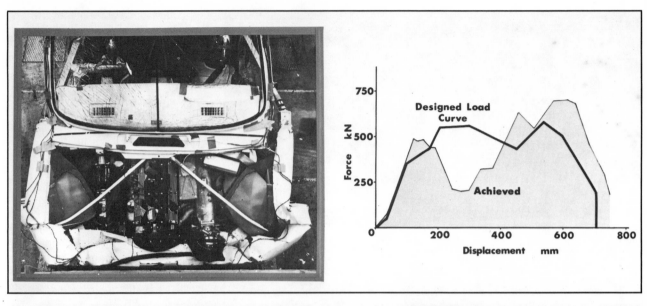

consist of 20 panels but has been replaced by a 'monoside' – one single major pressing from the windscreen pillar base to the back of the cabin. The inner door panel, formerly three pressings, is now one.

Apart from weight, another subject that has become of increasing concern to designers in the last decade is aerodynamics. Such has been the almost fanatical search for efficiency that, in my opinion, we have some very dull boxes on the road today, lacking any semblance of style or pleasing distinction. Jaguar is one company that has always stood for style and so I was particularly interested to hear Jim Randle's views on aerodynamics.

The style of the car has been paramount. All the clinic work we have ever done has said the car must be a Jaguar, must be elegant and traditional. So that has had to come first. Aerodynamic stability has always figured very highly in every car we have done and this car is no different. It has a lower drag than the car it replaces. It is not a trend setter on drag, on the other hand it has a low cross-sectional area, so in terms of total drag you will find the car is quite competitive.

I picked the project up with some seriousness in about '79 and started to do some work around the structures and the suspensions. We didn't start any serious work on the car until the Spring of 1980. Even then I was so strapped for people that for the first year I could only put thirteen on the car. We were trying to get Series III quality and reliability right and that had to be of prime importance.

Clearly we were in a very difficult state at

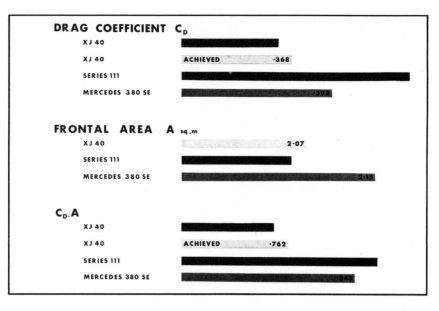

DRAG COEFFICIENT C_D

XJ 40		
XJ 40	ACHIEVED	·368
SERIES 111		
MERCEDES 380 SE		·39?

FRONTAL AREA A sq.m

XJ 40		2·07
SERIES 111		
MERCEDES 380 SE		2·1?

C_D.A

XJ 40		
XJ 40	ACHIEVED	·762
SERIES 111		
MERCEDES 380 SE		·84?

that time – we'd got no cash. The principal problem was surviving and we had to tackle the product we'd got, not the product that we hadn't got.

We didn't actually get enough Engineering headcount around us to do the job properly until August '84 and, at that point, we got to the headcount I had identified, as being required, in 1980. But of course we'd multiplied the complexity of the project, in terms of its quality and reliability achieve-

ments, some way by then. So we've always been chasing the headcount target all the way through this project.

Randle is not as openly critical of the BL management of this period as some of his colleagues and former colleagues.

They had their problems at that time. I think that some of the advice we got out of BL at that time was wrong. There were people in BL advising us that XJ40 was a dinosaur.

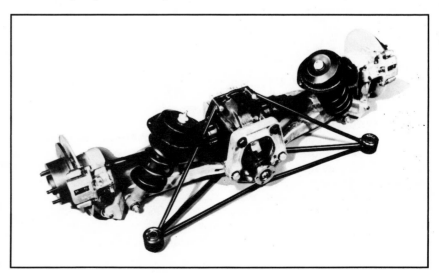

However there were some people, particularly Sir Michael Edwardes, who saw more than that.

In answer to my question about his role, Jim has this to say.

I guess I drove the whole project – for a while I think I was the only bloke who believed in it! I guess the thing that would go down to my credit would be particularly the rear suspension, and some of the front suspension. I was also involved in refining the style and the tyres.

The driven rear suspension is one of the most difficult parts of a motor car to get right because you have a number of inputs from things like gear contact meshing, engine firing order, and wheel inbalance into the system, yet you cannot mount the system very flexibly, because after all, it is controlling the car in terms of cornering power, and wind-up is a major problem. The careful development to ensure that you can do all of those things without getting yourself into one problem or another is very complex.

The Series III suspension is really a very competent piece of work done a very long time ago. In many respects it's geometrically inaccurate, but like the bumblebee that shouldn't fly, it actually does and does very well. With XJ6 we set out with a different suspension to the one that it eventually had. We tried to do some of the things then, that we have now done on the XJ40 suspension.

This other suspension [mentioned in Bob Knight's reports in Chapter 2] was an inclined wishbone suspension to give anti-dive, anti-squat, very much as XJ40 currently is and, in fact, one or two of the elements carry over to XJ40. It was mounted into the body as does the XJ40 set-up, but its major failing was that it was located at the front by a torque tube, the resonant behaviour of which we never got under proper control. By 1967 we just couldn't overcome the overrun boom resonances that we were getting, they were really quite severe, and it was due purely to cantilever resonance of the nose of the diff.

So eventually we decided the only way to get the car into production, was to put in

the suspension that we knew and loved.

I've forgotten how many suspensions I've designed in the meantime trying to do better, which was not easy, but it took me a long time, I've done everything – complete torque tubes through the car, all sorts of mounting systems, and so on.

The suspension we have under XJ40 is the best I have been able to do in some twenty years working on this subject. It does manage by dint of its design to isolate one set of requirements from another.

Also on XJ40 we have had to design an entirely new electrical system to achieve the levels of reliability. That has been a monumental task.

To put the problems into perspective, total annual warranty cost worldwide on the Series III at this time was £7.6m. The average number of faults per car was 15.85 and the cost per car was £540.

The area generating the most cost was paint rectification with 21 per cent of the total, but electrical and instrument faults accounted for a staggering 35 per cent and was the biggest percentage. The total number of faults was 2.3 times those of the Mercedes 'S' class and 1.4 times the 6/700 Series BMW. Paint faults were no less than 22 times that for BMW and five times more than Mercedes, whilst electrical faults were eight times that of Mercedes and twice that of BMW.

Talk of automotive electrics brings in Peter Scholes, who describes himself as a Jaguar man by adoption having worked at Rover, BL and BL Technology before joining Jaguar in early 1981.

I was brought in when they were looking to bring about a change in order to introduce reliability into the vehicle electrical systems from the concept stage.

I was pleasantly surprised because they were further down the road with the new model than I'd anticipated and I was particularly surprised how far in advance of other vehicle manufacturers at that time the concept of the '40' was. It amazed me how much such a small team had achieved and I

think it was this dedication which was one of the key points that turned Jaguar round.

So I came into that sort of atmosphere, but I found that, although there was a specification for the electrics and electronics, it was very loose. They had a styled mock-up vehicle but didn't know how to go about controlling it, switching or interfacing systems because there was only limited electrical expertise here at that time. So it was really a case of going back to an almost clean piece of paper in what was then a totally unrealistic timescale. The date for launch at that time was about two and a half years away. For someone to look at a vehicle electrical system, design it, take it all through the testing and sign-off, in a company that was fighting for its life, was almost impossible. In hindsight, had I been less enthusiastic at the time, I would have said it was impossible!

The styling clinics were giving the company some indications on aesthetics but the man in the street is not really interested in the more technical aspects of the electrical system. He is not bothered how something is operated. His only concern is that it works every time:

So I literally got this clean sheet of paper and said 'Let's re-write the rules'. If we look at the BLS, the British Leyland Standards, they were really evolved for mass production vehicles with very little electrical and electronic input into them. They use off-the-shelf equipment, to a degree, and wherever something different was required, it was left to the supplier to do the design. I felt that if I adopted the same principles here, all I would be doing would be perpetuating the standards that had been accepted in the past by all except the customer who was demanding a higher level of reliability.

I looked at the MIL (Military) Standards to see what we could adopt for automotive practices. There is a big problem here in that the Military have massive budgets. They can spend an awful lot of money to design, develop and achieve objectives but if you equate that to the automotive industry, there isn't a company in the world

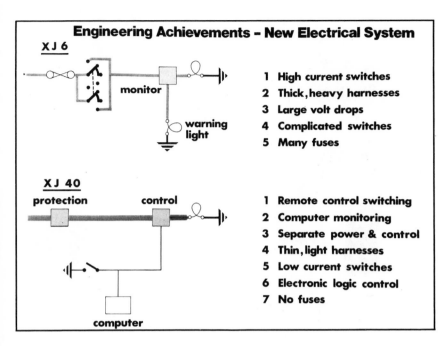

Engineering Achievements - New Electrical System

XJ 6

monitor

warning light

1 High current switches
2 Thick, heavy harnesses
3 Large volt drops
4 Complicated switches
5 Many fuses

XJ 40

protection   control

computer

1 Remote control switching
2 Computer monitoring
3 Separate power & control
4 Thin, light harnesses
5 Low current switches
6 Electronic logic control
7 No fuses

Shown here is Engineering's graphical representation of the arguments for the new electrical system that was being considered in 1980. (J.C.)

that could obtain that amount of money to achieve that level of reliability.

So I retained the principles of the Military Standards and evolved the Jaguar electrical product and test specifications, which were very rigid, so that we could achieve this reliability. We could then identify that if we wanted a vehicle to last 15 years, or whatever figure we required, we could then design an item, but not only design it, we could bring about the testing regime to prove it. Thus we could have the confidence that we could always achieve this, and it changed the whole philosophy. Even something as simple as a lamp. I would not accept the principle that they were batch tested at a supplier. To me that wasn't good enough because what I wanted was to get a 100 per cent guarantee that whatever was taken out of a pallet and put on our vehicle, would meet all our design parameters.

That meant changing not only the concept of design, tests and test specifications, but also the thinking and controls at suppliers in order to eliminate component infant mortality in the field.

We set a standard that some British

suppliers absolutely shuddered at and said was unattainable. They reckoned we would bankrupt Jaguar and any supplier who went along with us. I think it was a tragedy, in those early days, that a lot of British companies took that attitude because it did force me, unfortunately, to look abroad where these principles were already being practised. We have pulled a lot back to British companies now though.

So that was the first major change – getting everybody going along with us and this had a knock-on effect in other areas. The same principles have been applied to the engine, body, trim and chassis, I think I could say, without fear of contradiction, that today we must have some of the highest standard of specifications in the industry, so much so that I could name two or three major companies in the world market who are now adopting our specs, and are ringing us daily to see if they can use them. It has also changed a lot of suppliers who are adopting the processes.

The major part of our work on the electrical system, modules and components will never ever be seen by the public but it will show itself up in a very reliable vehicle.

Having established the principle of reliability, attention turned to formulating an overall electrical philosophy for the vehicle. Not surprisingly in this computer age, microprocessors had a large part to play. Some seven systems exist together with logic-based technology.

We looked at the systems. The engine,

Wiring harnesses are placed wherever possible in protective channels as seen on the inner sill section. (J.C.)

management and ignition already had micro-electronics in that area so we expanded it and integrated both the fuelling and the ignition. We then looked at the driver-activated systems and tried to take out a lot of switching operations to reduce driver fatigue – such things as turning the heated rear window on and off, which we made automatic through a processor. Thus a number of the timing functions evolved around a central microprocessor system – we were probably the first people to do that – so anything of a real-time base or driver interface goes through the central processor. That then gave two systems.

It was logical to utilise a microprocessor to make the air conditioning system far more efficient so there is a very sophisticated air conditioning system without the sophistication of operation by the driver – it's very simple, but very effective. Then you start looking at cruise control which is very popular in the States. So that has its own stand-alone processor based system. We also brought in ABS braking which is another processor-based system.

Scholes makes the point that it was necessary to have so many separate systems and processors simply because in those days the manufacturers were always working in isolation and nobody manufactured one all embracing system. So it was necessary to design systems to stand alone in isolation. For example, there could be enough capacity in the engine management ECU (electronic control unit) to handle the cruise control but they are made by two different suppliers from two different continents. The ideal is an integrated system but in the time available it was not possible to achieve that for the XJ40, but it will come.

This necessary compromise brings another problem:

Do you develop half a dozen pieces of test equipment, which in themselves can be very expensive, and expect all your dealers to purchase them?. Ideally not, so the next stage is to develop a system so that you can test the whole of the vehicle and have software changes for any model variants.

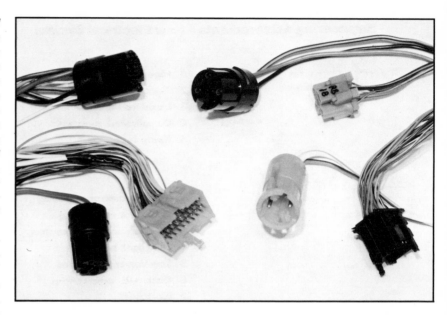

A great deal of time and investment went into designing new connectors that could withstand all conditions and perform reliably day in, day out. (J.C.)

Below: The dash panel does not appear to have changed greatly from this mock-up created in 1980. (J.C.)

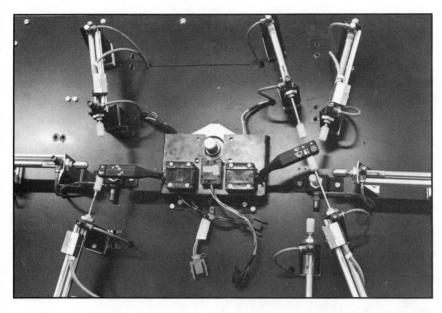

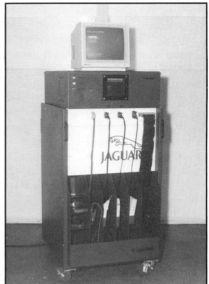

Testing rigs, such as this one continuouly operating the stalk controls, have been used to check durability of many of the components employed in the XJ40. (J.C.)

The 32 x 32 dot matrix screen, which provides a grid for displaying warning symbols, and central micro processor justify Randle's comment that the XJ40 is a computer on wheels. (J.C.)

This single piece of equipment, the computer based Jaguar Diagnostic System, can investigate and diagnose faults in the whole electrical system and will be compulsory equipment for all dealers.

Then you can specify that this must be installed by all your dealers. This became known as the JDS (Jaguar Diagnostic System).

So the system started to embrace more than just the vehicle. We then looked at certain on-board diagnostics as well and this is another processor based system. This brings up the question of how much information a driver can take in when he is driving down a motorway or through a town. A dot matrix and alpha numeric display achieves a satisfactory interface for the warning symbols, etc.

The clinics indicated that Jaguar owners conservatively wished to retain some traditional instrumentation. There is consequently a mixture of analogue instruments for mph and rpm, and vacuum fluorescent bar charts for more minor information.

The overriding question then is, how do we operate all the functions? We couldn't really go to multiplexing because as I think the Press have said a few times now – indeed every time I read a paper on multiplexing – it's still five years away. People have been saying it's five years away for possibly the last fifteen! However, I couldn't afford to be innovative and the first in the field when I was still suffering from lack of expertise here. So what we have done is evolved what we term the 'low current earth line switching' system which is possibly unique and is the stage before multiplexing.

[Multiplexing, for those who are not au fait with the term, is a means of transmitting different signals down the same piece of wire. Thus one ring, or 'H'. main can serve a number of different items.]

Instead of signals going down a multiplexed wire, what we have is a number of wires carrying the individual message to the various areas for activation. You still have a harness but by tuning the size of the cable to the signal, which can be anything

The rough, unforgiving tracks and relentless dust of the Australian outback provided an extremely harsh regime in which to thoroughly prove the XJ40. (J.C.)

from 10 milliamps up to 200 milliamps, the amount of copper, the size of cable, can be reduced dramatically. This enables you to put in 30 to 40 per cent more features for the same space and weight. We have actually achieved a very high specification with a lighter harness.

That still provides a challenge because it has got to go all round the world from –40°C in Canada to +50°C in Death Valley, California which the same vehicle could be going through, literally, days later. So we applied the same philosophy to the cable and connectors as we did to all the electronics and other equipment. Again we found it was very hard to find a company that would accept this very tough standard. We ended up doing a high percentage of in-house tests ourselves and we've evolved cable specifications that are now being used progressively by the automotive industry.

It wasn't easy when you bear in mind that you can snap conventional cable and plastic like a matchstick at –30°C, before you even get down to –40°C. That was one side of it. The other side was that we couldn't find any connectors that met our standards. It's a very harsh environment under the bonnet which, with a vehicle travelling at speed on hard packed ice in Canada, is subjected to something akin to sandblasting thrown up from the wheels. You also get a similar reaction off the back roads in, say, Australia.

Eventually we homed in on one supplier and between us we have tooled up a whole new range of connectors. They have anti-back-out and throw-apart features, so that if it isn't fully pushed home it throws itself apart. Once it goes past the point of no return, it pulls itself in and locks. We also have waterproof and non-waterproof versions of the same type of connector, which isn't easy when you think of the differential rates of expansion of the different materials going from cold climates to hot.

We are very confident that we now have a specification that is worldwide, with high reliability for our customer.

The next items to be addressed were switches. Base metal switches have a

finite life and are a common source of failure. With the new systems, however, the switches needed only to carry a low current as they were merely acting as inputs to a processor. A domed metal foil clicker plate contact on a printed circuit board formed the switch element. By utilising precious metals and applying a membrane over the assembly to prevent moisture ingress and deterioration, the switches have a longer life. But as the public is not yet ready for switches lacking any feel, a tactile element is provided to the clicker plate.

That's very nice when you are switching driver interface, but you've still got to switch a load, a motor or lights – the inrush current of a 55 watt headlamp shoots way up for those few milliseconds until it drops off.

Transistor switching was looked at but, at the time, this was not considered to be the answer for higher current items.

For higher currents the most cost effective and reliable route is the old electromechanical relay. So we called in a number of relay manufacturers and said that we wanted to go back to first principles because we were going to use relays on just about every switching application – even on an indicator which might see twelve million cycles on the life of a car. We stated that we didn't think the off-the-shelf relays you are selling are good enough for these applications to the reliability level that we require.

We wrote a relay specification in conjunction with BL Technology, because I didn't have all the expertise, and sent it to eleven manufacturers around the world. We ended up with three companies that said, 'some of our relays will meet this spec, but we've never seen a spec like this before. It will mean a lot of redesign and testing!'

The programme lasted two and a half years and two manufacturers have said to us that we have probably moved relay design forward five or seven years. At present we have just one supplier who can meet every part of the spec but because

other companies are looking at this earth line low current and remote high current switching system – it's no secret that some of our competitors are now looking at it – so the market for relays is expanding and they can see a number of manufacturers going over to this specification. So with a bit of luck we shall have a wider choice in the future pending the improvement in high current solid state switching.

So this again gives us reliability. I want to emphasize this, because this is where I came in. I will not compromise. I would rather walk out of the automotive industry than compromise on reliability. What I have stressed to all my team is that the customer comes first and our main objective must always be reliability.

It is most important to remember that the XJ40 is a totally new car with literally nothing carried over. The engine, body design and construction, electrics and electronics, suspensions, transmissions are all new, or at least new to Jaguar. Bearing this in mind, plus the fanatical search for reliability, plus the desire to sell this car worldwide, development took on an immense importance. Rig resting would begin to play an increasing part as time passed, but without such facilities, it meant subjecting vehicles to every form of test in every possible extreme of climate and conditions.

Malcolm Oliver has been the XJ40 Project Manager for Engineering.

Derek Waelend was brought in as Project Director before moving on to his present position as Manufacturing Director and Jim Randle, our Director of Product Engineering, takes a very personal interest in XJ40 – it is the most important project we have ever done. So he has made the technical decisions principally. My role has been, primarily, to ensure that all the development work has been done, that the parts are satisfactory, that test work has been carried out, and to feedback all the problems, making sure that all the right people know about the problems, wherever they may occur.

I have also had a substantial involvement

setting up all the durability testing because XJ40, without any question, is the most tested car we have ever made.

We have substantially increased our rig test facility. It was very modest and we used to test very small numbers of our components. In any rig test programme you have got to build up a benchmark to say that that rig test specification will reproduce what happens on a car, and if it's OK on the rig then you can be confident it will be OK on the car. We did not have that depth of experience, so we tested cars as well.

We set up a programme whereby we used production cars known as SDV's (specially designated vehicles), which merely means they're early built cars which have an allocation or task which is not to be sold – that ranges from Engineering cars to Photographic cars.

Jaguar Rover Australia, at that time part of the same company, carried out the durability testing in that continent.

We had a very good relationship with them. For our winter testing we used a site at Timmins in Ontario in conjunction with Jaguar Canada. We now hire workshops, which we have equipped, over there and run durability tests out of there using local drivers. The interesting thing is the word just passes round that we want some drivers and at least 70 per cent of the applicants are female. Put an advert in a paper here and you're unlikely to get a woman apply.

We ran anything from six to eight cars during one winter, aiming to achieve during the period of December through to the end of March, 50,000 miles on each car. All this was with a view to comparing the environmental performance with that which we'd measured in environmental chambers – cold rooms, hot rooms, etc.

The testing in Canada began in 1983. About a year before this Richard Cresswell went out to the States and set up a site to run the then current cars in Phoenix in Summer and, initially, go up to Canada in Winter. After a while he became based in Phoenix where

Jaguar built a permanent workshop. There they had six durability cars plus one additional car on which to try things. There is also a Mercedes 300 to see what the competition is like!

We also [continues Oliver] make use of Jaguar Inc.'s facility at New Jersey where we run a small number of cars. They just run round New York basically, not doing many miles, in fact they do less than a thousand miles a week. Whereas cars in Timmins, in spite of the ice covered roads,

By mid-April, 1985 no less than one million miles of durability testing had been covered 'down under'. (J.C.)

will average 4 to 5,000 miles a week. We've now modified that to include cold start tests.

Cold start testing consists of leaving cars out over night in conditions as low as –40°C and then expecting them to start immediately!

In Phoenix we were running 3,500 to 4,000 miles per week with just two shifts a day. In Australia we average between 4,000 and 5,000 miles per week with three shifts using a combination of dirt roads and normal highways. But we did an additional test at a place called Cobar, which is 700

km West of Sydney, and there it is all dirt roads. We set out there to run 35,000 miles on two cars with no major structural problems. We attempted that having completed pavé testing here at MIRA and we achieved it on both cars.

We went to Oman in '85 and did 50,000 miles on each of two cars. The Middle East market is particularly sensitive in terms of believing in a product. They will only do so once they have seen it and know it's been in that environment.

The high speed testing was done at the giant circular track at Nardo in Southern Italy. Richard Cresswell

enthuses about the venue. 'It's simply the best track of its kind in the world. It is virtually eight miles around and I understand that speeds well in excess of 200 mph have been run round there. Ferrari certainly test cars at over 170. To all intents and purposes it is a straight road. All banked tracks have a neutral steer speed. MIRA is about 80/85 mph, whereas Nardo is about 140!'

Norman Dewis, who retired in 1985 after more than 30 years of sterling service, to be succeeded by Cresswell, recalls that the early cars were actually found to be quicker with their camouflage than without!

The programme at Nardo progressively built-up. In 1982 FEP3 was taken down for six weeks. Several months later the Jaguar team went down again and with minor problems it was taking six weeks to clock up 25,000 miles. By 1986 the testers were there for the full year and achieving the same mileage in just four weeks.

Latterly they have been testing engine variants and catalyst cars for it will not be long before the catalyst version becomes more common than the non-catalyst cars with stricter emission regulations becoming more widespread. As Oliver explains:

The objective is to achieve an average between 85 and 90 per cent of the car's maximum speed. So a 3.6 automatic European specification non-catalyst car has a maximum speed of 136 mph, therefore we would set out to average around 120 mph. It is a cycle though, not just a matter of driving at 120 mph. There are several cycles of lifting off and slowing down to 70 mph followed by full throttle accelerations. Some laps are completed at maximum speed. It all builds up a picture.

Our target for the life of a car is 150,000 miles or 12 years – it doesn't mean, though, that on that day it self destructs!

Basically, we're looking for 99% reliability for every component over that time. In the UK, as well as normal road testing, we've principally done specialist tests, such as pavé. There has always been an industry

equation that 100 miles on the pavé equals 10,000 miles of normal use. We started off doing 1,000 miles on the pavé and later increased that to 1,250, the equivalent of a 125,000 mile life. We also do what we call a G40 test, which we do at Gaydon. It is a combination of Third World type roads and a little high speed running on their emission circuit, which because it has a lot of corners, gives a lot of throttle on, throttle off work.

There are reversing cycles, steering pad work and going over what is called the LSE. That is a sequence of special road surfaces, for instance, manhole covers, broken concrete blocks, tree roots, white lines, reverse camber, severe camber narrow roads, sleeping policemen – all this combined but very condensed. We do 35,000 miles of that which we reckon equates to 150,000 normal miles.

On durability testing we have now done over 5,500,000 miles in the last three and a half years.

> Extensive running on the pavé is jarring work for the drivers but good proving for the vehicle showing up any defects far sooner than would the ordinary road. (J.C.)

> Insert: Even when pavé testing is in private at such places as MIRA and Gaydon the XJ40s wore their camouflage. (J.C.)

During that mileage, some 3,400 problems have been identified and solved. Combustion problems, for example, showed up during the initial high speed work but also included amongst that list were items that Manufacturing wanted changing in order to standardise or make construction easier.

A major area in which we learnt a lesson was with our front suspension beam. The

front suspension is very much the same principle as Series III where you have a rubber-mounted beam which in turn carries the engine. What we wanted to do was try and reduce the weight and so we decided to go to two complex pressings instead of a completely built up structure which was effective but an expensive and labour-intensive item.

We decided firstly to try some handmade ones and they were just totally unsuccessful. We had something that looked like a front suspension but literally when you put the weight of the car on they started to bend, or would certainly deflect. Once we started running the car, cracking occurred all over the place. So we went next to a low cost tool to press them and put some, but not all, the form into them. But there was still too much hand working in that and we then started putting some reinforcement, and therefore weight, into it. We did FE (finite element) analysis on the structure and correlated some of the high stress points. This was all new technology to us and to assist us we used BL Technology, which is now known as Gaydon Technology, or colloquially as Gaytech!

'We introduced some form changes but never got out of some of the problems until we actually got the off-tools parts. The lesson we learned there was that it would have been far better to have put in the £100,000 and have had some proper 'soft' tools made and produced pressings. That caused us an awful lot of sleepless nights.'

In the five and a half million miles only two cars have been written off and nobody has been injured. Inevitably there have been incidents as Malcolm Oliver recalls.

In Australia the XJ40 enemy number one is the wombat – a wombat is a block of concrete on legs! They can wipe the front off, or the spoiler at the very least. On average, at night, we were unfortunately hitting one a month, and obviously you hit the odd kangaroo!

In Canada the cars slip off the road once a week regularly, which is hardly surprising

The front suspension remained largely unchanged in principle with most work being directed at reducing the weight and manufacturing time of the crossmember. (J.C.)

considering the mileage we are doing. They generally have a soft landing fortunately. Once, though, we were filming in Arizona with two cars running in echelon and there was a slight rise followed by a turn to the left. The second car, in the dust, didn't pick out quick enough that there was a bank ahead, and although it was just dirt it had been baked like concrete and unfortunately it hit that!

I remember another amusing incident. In a few years time we are going over to German Teves brakes and dropping Girling. Two years ago, when we started the project with Teves, and Girling were unaware of our co-operation with their competitors, the truck delivering a development car to Teves was uncertain where to go. The story has it that Girling, at that time, were testing an XJ40 in Germany and the car was parked in one of the rest areas on an autobahn when up came the lorry driver and says, 'Oh, I've got one of those cars in the back – any idea where this Teves place is?'

We had a rude letter from BMW. We were testing on the Gross Glockner and a photograph appeared of an XJ40 in its camouflage in, I think, Motor. Some of the Girling lads, who were doing the testing, had got hold of some Mini chrome beading, bent it into kidney shapes, reminiscent of a certain grille, and put it on to the front!

Rig testing has grown throughout the project and will assume an even greater importance in the future. A separate rig design and manufacturing department was set up and some 94 special rigs have been built amongst which is a 'four-poster' electro-hydraulic rig to simulate the vibrations and stresses of road and proving ground surfaces. Furthermore, another 384 rigs have been constructed, sometimes by Jaguar, and used by suppliers for testing components.

Richard Cresswell feels the value will be felt by,

Testing rigs, such as this one for wishbones, were to have been used much earlier in the project and would have saved considerable time. (J.C.)

Development having a much more usable prototype car early on. One of the things that was difficult about XJ40 was that in the early days, so many things were lashed up that it was hard to objectively assess what the car was going to be like.

A lot of it you just had to forget because that wasn't how it was going to be. The external appearance was unchanged but a lot of the mechanical bits and pieces that went into it weren't what we have finished up with at all. They were just put on to make the car a runner.

As a further testing aid, a strange 'vehicle' was constructed and became known as the 'beach buggy'. George Mason explains the reasoning behind it:

It is purely and simply a tubular steel chassis just to carry all the components in exactly the same positions as in the car and weighted to give exactly the same weight per wheel as on the car. To that end that vehicle has now so many miles on the pavé it's unbelievable. The actual chassis itself hasn't fatigued in any way, 'cause it's rather

brick built to put it mildly!

If you were to put an axle in a car to test it and do 1,000 miles of pavé, you'd virtually ruin the whole of the car. Put it on the 'beach buggy', do 1,000 miles and all you've hurt is the axle.

The other thing we did was we built it open, originally, so that the co-driver could swivel round and actually view the rear suspension working or remove the front wing and watch the front working. The rear suspension is a complex thing and not a lot of people understand it, watching all this

compliance at work. The trouble was that if you put it under a normal motor car and went and did a test and had a failure you would not know for sure why this had happened. Rig testing then came along but that is only simulation rather than in the actual car, so this 'beach buggy' came in between, and that's one vehicle that's really earned its corn.

It was finished about Christmas '82 and soon manifested itself as to what a good thing it was. If we'd built ourselves two or three of those, we would have saved an awful lot of time.

By launch, the 'buggy' had covered some 7,332 miles, or the equivalent of seven normal car pavé tests! Nor is it in retirement now because it is being used on further development work. A total of 89 SDVs were used solely by Engineering on work around the world.

The XJ40 is fitted with the TD wheel-tyre system developed by Dunlop and manufactured by them and, under licence, Michelin. The TD rim has a special groove in which the TD tyre bead is locked ensuring that, in

The 'buggy' with its massively strong old-fashioned chassis allowed components to be tested for a greater mileage than any modern monocoque body could be expected to withstand. (J.C.)

the event of a puncture, the tyre stays
on its seat and that an exposed wheel
rim does not dig into the road surface.
Inside the tyre is a sealant gel which is
capable of sealing small punctures and
reducing the rate of air loss in larger
ones. Jaguar and Dunlop believe that
between 65 and 70 per cent of all
punctures will be sealed by the gel.

Tom Holmes, who is Manager of
Advanced Tyre Development with
Dunlop, mentions that,

*this is not Jaguar's first experience of the
tyre as it is fitted to the XJR-6 sports racing
car. The tyre development has been carried
out in conjunction with Jaguar engineers.
Jaguar and ourselves have virtually lived
together on the tyre/suspension/handling
characteristics of the car. It's really been a
joint effort from the start with testing at
Nardo on high speed and we've probably
been brought in more than any other
manufacturer of components.*

*Noise is always a factor with modern
high performance cars, particularly with a
quiet car like the Jaguar with a very good
suspension. Noise intrusion is very dramatic if you get it wrong.*

*Engineering it out is done by reposition-
ing the segments and generally changing
the tread compounds. It is a long hard slog,
basically!*

A great deal of work has, not surprisingly, been done with outside suppliers
but not only with the manufacturers.
Several universities have been heavily
involved, an example being Loughbo-
rough University who have assisted in
the design of the XJ40 seats.

The XJ40 interior styling was considerably revised during the project.
The thinking in the early eighties was
that the traditional leather and veneers
were no longer appropriate to the
computer. age. Furthermore, plastics
would be lighter, easier and cheaper to
produce, and above all cost less in
themselves. Believe it or not it was the
Americans, usually the leaders in all
that is modern and trendy, who told
Jaguar management very firmly that
they were not impressed.

The styling clinics, which are
discussed in more detail in Chapter 7,
also conveyed this message and between the middle and end of 1984 as
major a redesigning as was still
possible was undertaken. Geof Lawson, who had joined the company as
Chief Stylist in the Spring of 1984, was
immediately asked to come up with a
Trim Enhancement Programme.
Wherever possible the tasteless plastic
was thrown out and tradition returned.
That Lawson and his colleague, Colin
Holtum, did a good job can clearly be
seen in the finished product that won
the notable distinction of being considered an improvement over Series

Originally the idea was to make the
conventional automatic transmission
shift into a 'U' shape. (J.C.)

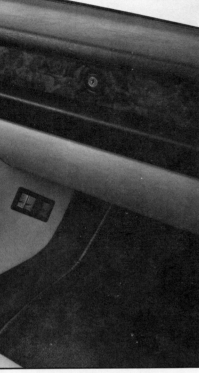

This is an interior mock-up done in 1980. Thankfully it was decided to return to a more traditional interior with less plastic and more real wood. (J.C.)

III.   On a different topic, concerning an innovation the 1981 White Book says: *A new concept is proposed for this model designed to overcome the difficulties created by the additional gear position of the four speed (automatic) gearbox and also to ensure that the criticisms levelled at our present gearchange are overcome. In order to increase the spacing between the functions, the change gate has now become a 'U' rather than a slot, thus the travel is increased by a factor of two. By this means all the driving functions can be placed on one side of the 'U' whilst all the manoeuvring and parking functions are on the other side.*

The above describes the early thoughts on what has changed from a 'U' to a 'J' and become known as the 'J Gate', or unofficially after its originator, the 'Randle Handle'!

During the mid-eighties, the XJ40 became the automotive industry's best known, or worst kept, secret. The launch appeared imminent for a couple of years and various dates were mentioned in the Press from time to time. Jim Randle explains the truth behind the rumours.

The idea for a rather different automatic transmission selector evolved into the 'J' gate. (J.C.)

In 1980 we had a company that was going out of business and we were told that if we didn't have a new motor car in the market place, we'd had it. So we sold the car on the understanding that we could put it in

CAD (computer aided design) is an invaluable asset in ensuring the accuracy of information produced and allows easy and speedy modification of designs. Not a great deal of the XJ40 was designed with the aid of CAD but gradually all data is being put on to computer and future updates will be achieved by this means. (J.C.)

the market place by the back end of 1983, which was ridiculous, absolutely ridiculous.

I asked Jim if he believed it then.

Well, we knew we had a programme that if we got it right first time, it would work. We ain't that clever.

But if we hadn't sold it on that plan, we wouldn't have sold it all. If we'd said, 'Look, we really need five or six years to do this job, the BL Board would have laughed us out of court and we wouldn't have got anything. So, sure, we were kidding ourselves, if you like. We were assuming we could do a better job than, perhaps, we'd ever done before, which didn't happen. The mistake we made was in delaying it in short lumps. If you do that you can't make a major change, you've got to do a little bit of a change. It would have been better in hindsight to say it isn't really good enough, let's give ourselves another couple of years. We got there eventually, but it probably took a year longer as a result than it would have done if we'd taken a big step to start with.

Taking into account our miniscule facilities compared to our competition, we have taken the same time or less than the competition – Mercedes take seven or nine years – and I believe we've produced a product which is . . . competitive. The world will judge that.

To a degree we went through a fair bit of British muddle, but as is typical of the British, we came out not too badly in the end.

It is an impossibility to describe and do justice to the hundreds, or thousands, of people and their work in the design and development of the XJ40 in a mere few thousand words. I was with Jim Randle on the day the first car rolled off the No. 1 production line and as we walked down the track, he pointed out various items, enthusing about their virtues. To complete this look at the technical side of the car, I conclude with some edited highlights of our conversation:

The front suspension is like the Series III

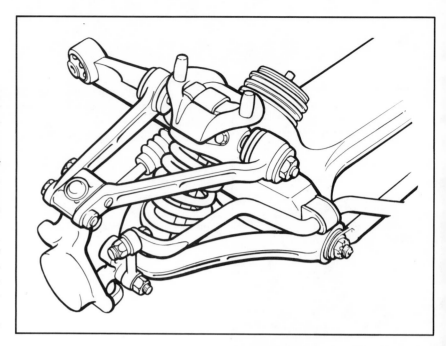

Front suspension wishbones and uprights are forged steel with the wishbone pivots angled to provide anti-dive characteristics. (J.C.)

except that it has been, if you like, productionized. There is no adjustment in the system, it's all built and then bored so that it's dead accurate. We don't have to adjust the camber or anything like that.

The rear suspension is really quite unique, with a floating lower wishbone hung on a pendulum plate, with a duplex mounting system at the back, so that it's got a very low fore and aft resonant frequency below wheel balance which gives it lots of attenuation. It's mounted almost at the roll centre height so there's virtually no parasitic roll during cornering, it

maintains its height. It's arranged so that the forces transmitted from the wheel through the damper system appear at the front, so that as you accelerate the weight is transferred, it pushes the nose down, whilst the torque is trying to wind it up. The result is that the final movement is relatively low and you can go for very soft mounting systems which still control the car whilst attenuating the noise. It's all patented now!

[Talking next of the bumpers.] The US Federal car looks just like a European car

The new rear suspension incorporates an unique pendulum arrangement which allows fore and aft movement of the lower wishbone inner fulcrum, but which maintains very high natural stiffness. (J.C.)

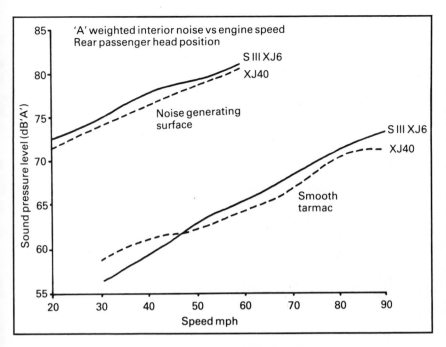

'A' weighted interior noise vs engine speed
Rear passenger head position

Graph: Sound pressure level (dB'A') vs Speed mph

S III XJ6
XJ40
Noise generating surface
S III XJ6
XJ40
Smooth tarmac

---

but it still manages the 5 mph impact, and upon impact it all slides underneath the car. There is a large channel in there and it's all cammed on the outside and pivots at each front corner so that as it goes back the sides of the bumper lift out and clear the wheels.

Moving on Jim pointed out, with a chuckle, the damper action on the

> The air conditioning unit is a completely new design and includes a solar sensor to adjust for sudden external changes in temperature – like the sun coming out! (J.C.)

> Jaguar engineers are almost fanatical about noise and go to enormous lengths to engineer out all such impediments to relaxed driving. (J.C.)

ashtrays, a neat little touch, and mentioned that with regard to the electrics, the connectors alone cost £73 per car.

The body's a fairly clean thing. There are only 325 panels in this one against 621 in the Series III. We were in all sorts of trouble with the crush tubes and I finished up foregoing my Christmas holidays in '81 and

working over at Park Sheet Metal and making them so that we could test them as soon as the people came back – yet another of my holidays that I gave up!

We can make it a lot stronger should legislation ever demand it.

The air conditioning unit is all micro processor controlled driven by stepping motors and it doesn't use conventional flaps, it uses barrel valves. Two units do the whole lot whereas conventionally you need four flaps. It's quite sophisticated and extremely reliable. It has been a combined development with Delanair and arrives pre-assembled. It not only has face level temperatures, it has a selection of three modes – the heater is automatic as well, by the way – but it also has a selection of humidities you can choose. You can have either manual or automatic modes. Even the simplest spec is pretty damn sophisticated.

[Looking at the window frames.] The lower line models have black with chrome outlines and the superior models have stainless steel. I've always thought that stainless steel upper frames were very much the hallmark of an elegant top of the market car.

There are three fuse boxes. If you get a failure in any one of them, it is indicated and tells you which box the failure is in and you don't have to go running round the car to find it.

The central door locking switch is different – when you hit that it shuts all the windows as well!

It really is a box of computers on wheels.

Apart from being a highly gifted engineer and taking overall responsibility for design and development, Jim Randle also has to manage his ever-growing team. It is most interesting and encouraging to hear him talking of his colleagues.

You have to remember that people here, particularly in Engineering, are very dedicated to the company, they really are. They would deny it to a man, I have no doubt, but in fact they have tremendous loyalty.

It is very much a family atmosphere,

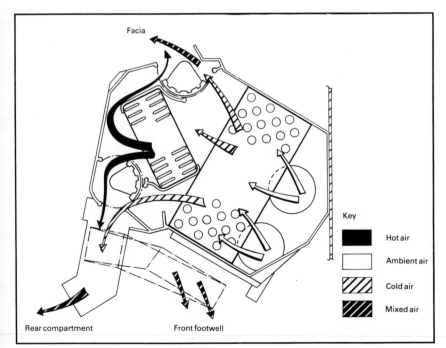

Facia

Key

Hot air

Ambient air

Cold air

Mixed air

Rear compartment   Front footwell

particularly those of us who have been around a long time. They are so committed to the product that they get quite emotionally involved in the cars. If you've got a problem, those lads will work through the night, night after night. You don't really have to ask them, they are those sort of people.

This isn't a company created by people. In some ways it is a company that creates people.

I'm very much aware of that when I am interviewed. It would be very easy to get things out of kilter, to think what a clever bugger I am. But it's not the case. The image of the company is enormous and it sometimes creates bigger people than they really are. It's those lads out there who create the motor car by their dedication.

Jim Randle, for whom the new XJ6s are a personal triumph, has masterminded the design since the beginning of the decade. (J.C.)

Chapter 5
Eighties Engines

During the last forty years, Jaguar have only really designed and built, in quantity, two basic engines. These are, of course, the famous XK, in a multitude of forms and sizes, and the superb V12.

As is well known the XK unit proved to be a legendary one and built and sustained the company's very reputation and fortunes. Its versatility has been, arguably, unmatched. In the early seventies it was joined by the sophisticated and silky smooth V12. This engine has never been built in the numbers envisaged due entirely to the unforeseeable fuel crises that afflicted the decade and whose effects carried over into the eighties.

Both have been proved on the race tracks of the world with the XK carrying the flag at Le Mans and in many other forms of racing since 1949. More latterly the V12 has had a chance to show its merits on the world's circuits.

In the early seventies, however, it was realised that the XK engine, brilliant though it was, was not surprisingly becoming a little long in the tooth. Furthermore as the decade progressed it was realised that the V12 was too thirsty even in HE form with heads incorporating the principles of Swiss engineer, Michael May. Even

The venerable XK engine is too well known to need further introduction, being arguably the most versatile power unit ever produced by any company and sustaining Jaguar Cars for nearly 40 years. (J.C.)

with the 20 per cent improvement in consumption this engendered, it was decided that the V12's life was limited and a new family of engines must power the Jaguars of the eighties and beyond.

In arriving at these conclusions, the engineers led by Harry Mundy (for those great gentlemen Bill Heynes, Claude Baily and Wally Hassan had by now retired), had experimented on engines related to the '12'. Although Jaguar stated at the time of the V12 launch that, 'it is relatively easy to derive a substantially smaller engine from the design,' this did not prove to

be so in practice.

It was further stated that the vee engine tooling cost represented an expenditure of £3m (the equivalent today in financial terms of, say, £12m and in engine development terms of, say £40m) and the installation was 'geared to produce a future optimum of 1,000 major power unit components per 80-hour (two-shift) week, and it is possible to utilise the equipment to produce alternative capacities and configurations . . .'. Sadly this was to prove wildly optimistic but the intention had been to produce a V8 as well and the tooling was laid down for both from the start.

The V12 block line was a dedicated, purpose-built transfer machine for producing 60 degree V12 and V8 cylinder blocks. Bob Knight feels, 'it is a good

example of the futility of making such sophisticated and totally dedicated equipment for a relatively small volume manufacturer. The people who were dealing with this at Jaguar undoubtedly, at the time, did not realise the importance of providing for future flexibility. Flexibility in tooling is the name of the game'.

George Buck, former engine development engineer and now retired, recalls the various engines tried:

One could consider a V8 version of the same [V12] engine by just chopping off four cylinders from the back and it could be produced on the same transfer machinery. It would produce 3½ litres of engine which was very handy for an alternative lower capacity engine. In fact we made quite a few pucker V8 versions, at least one

of which we fitted to an early XJ6.

I thought it was a good concept. It was a very satisfying engine and was obviously very competitive because it was giving 200 bhp. It was a very able unit in the saloon and obviously gave you more space under the bonnet. What killed it was the fact that being a 60 degree vee, following on from the 12, you were in a situation where you'd got two four-cylinder engines in effect and because they were not at 90 degrees, you finished up having to cater for secondary out-of-balance forces.

Ultimately we were able to eliminate those completely by fitting separate balance shafts on but that was an added complication.

It has always been stated that this, then, precluded using the V12 lines, but Buck disagrees.

We could, but it was unacceptable to Bob

Knight. He felt he did not want to cater for this secondary out-of-balance problem. We could get rid of it by suitable insulation and at one stage, I think we'd get just about cured it but it was dropped, which is a shame.

It started off initially, the V8, by adapting one of the twin-cam V12 engines and simply altering the crankshaft. At this stage it was still in a V12 carcass.

The engine had a single plane crankshaft as used on four-cylinder engines. Bob Knight gives his views on the engine and his reasons for his opposition to it:

It had quite a good power output on two carburettors, but it sounded and felt like a medium sized four. It was the uneven firing which was the worst feature. What one heard was two cylinders firing quite close

together and then there was a longer interval before the next two were heard relatively close together, and so on. In spite of the twice engine speed balancers, which were tried to cure the 'secondary' balance problem, it still sounded like a four.

In recent years, some American engines have appeared which are V6's made off V8 tooling. The better ones were caused to have even firing intervals using flying webs between the big-ends. That basically solved the problem and, though they are not fully balanced, they are really quite acceptable.

Amongst the reasons for choosing to produce a single cam version was the consideration of underbonnet space, but as one can see, even in this form there is little to spare. This engine will be offered in a long wheelbase XJ40 a year or so after introduction of the sixes, but meanwhile will continue in the 'old' Series III body. (J.C.)

Unfortunately it would seem that few photographs exist of the various engines built during the seventies, but Roger Clinkscales kindly photographed the 'sawn off' slant six especially for this book. (J.C.)

Where you have two such narrow big-end bearings of large diameter, as on the '12', there is not room to use even the slenderest of flying webs to give even firing.

The V8 was abandoned in 1972 and in the same year 'half' a V12 was built. Buck observes:

Obviously it was thought that, since the V12 was successful, then half a V12, which would give you about 2.65 litres, would be a useful thing to have. Again you could make the thing on the same production line, use the same components, pistons, rods, and all you would need to change was the crank and block.

So the first slant six was a sawn off V12 and we made several of those. They even ran in XJ's in that form. It was quite a reasonable performing vehicle and quite economical so we did a lot of work on the testbed to arrive at the best combination of manifolding, air filtration, exhaust system and so on.

Trevor Crisp, Group Chief Engineer (Power Units) and the man who assumed Mundy's mantle upon his retirement, played a leading part in these developments. 'These engines were considered to be insufficiently powerful. We were quite limited on the engine capacity and just halving the 5.3 didn't really give us a big enough capacity in any case.'

So the stroke was increased from 70 mm to 90 mm. The height of the block was, therefore, increased. No way could be found, however, of accommodating even a moderate height increase using the V12 block line which was the whole point of the exercise. Buck states, though, that much of what was learnt with these engines was applied to the two-valve version of the production engine.

During the same period, with compe-

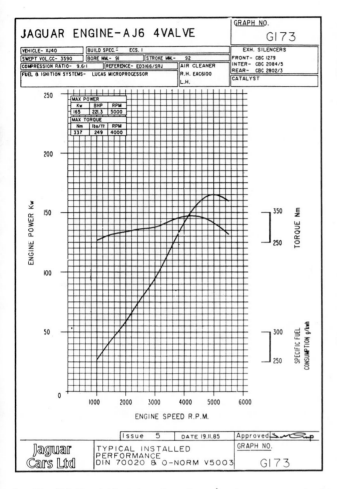

JAGUAR ENGINE—AJ6 4VALVE

GRAPH NO.
G173

VEHICLE- XJ40	BUILD SPEC.- ECS. 1		EXH. SILENCERS
SWEPT VOL.CC- 3590	BORE MM.- 91	STROKE MM.- 92	FRONT- CBC 1279
COMPRESSION RATIO- 9.6:1	REFERENCE- ED3166/SRJ	AIR CLEANER	INTER- CBC 2084/5
FUEL & IGNITION SYSTEMS- LUCAS MICROPROCESSOR	R.H. EAC6100 L.H.	REAR- CBC 2802/3

MAX POWER		
Kw	BHP	RPM
165	221.3	5000

MAX TORQUE		
Nm	lbs/ft	RPM
337	249	4000

Issue 5	DATE 19.11.85	Approved

Jaguar Cars Ltd	TYPICAL INSTALLED PERFORMANCE DIN 70020 & O-NORM V5003	GRAPH NO. G173

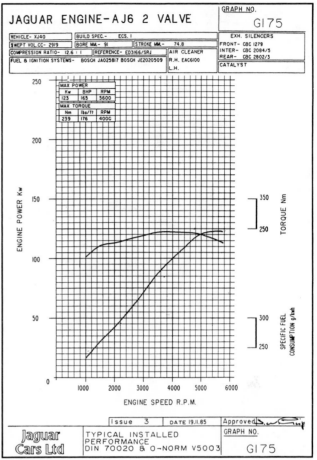

JAGUAR ENGINE—AJ6 2 VALVE

GRAPH NO.
G175

VEHICLE- XJ40	BUILD SPEC.- ECS. 1		EXH. SILENCERS
SWEPT VOL.CC- 2919	BORE MM.- 91	STROKE MM.- 74.8	FRONT- CBC 1279
COMPRESSION RATIO- 12.6:1	REFERENCE- ED3166/SRJ	AIR CLEANER	INTER- CBC 2084/5
FUEL & IGNITION SYSTEMS- BOSCH JA025817 BOSCH JE2020509	R.H. EAC6100 L.H.	REAR- CBC 2802/3 CATALYST

MAX POWER		
Kw	BHP	RPM
123	165	5600

MAX TORQUE		
Nm	lbs/ft	RPM
239	176	4000

Issue 3	DATE 19.11.85	Approved

Jaguar Cars Ltd	TYPICAL INSTALLED PERFORMANCE DIN 70020 & O-NORM V5003	GRAPH NO. G175

> The 3.6-litre AJ6 engine gives the relatively heavy XJ40 surprisingly good acceleration, a very healthy top speed, excellent torque and reasonable economy. (J.C.)

> The 2.9-litre is inevitably less lively but is a less complex, lower cost, unit that suits certain countries' tax regulations and is still a very respectable performer with fair economy. (J.C.)

tition thoughts in mind, a four-valve twin-cam V12 was constructed harnessing the great experience of Hassan and Mundy who had used such a configuration with international Grand Prix success during their days at Coventry Climax.

'We built', recalls George Buck, 'a comparatively highly tuned one and a medium tuned one. From memory with the lesser tuned one we were getting around 400 bhp but with the higher tuned version, which had 10.5:1 compression, a fair degree of overlap, high lift cams, tuned inlet and exhaust systems, we obtained 627 bhp and

there was undoubtedly more to come.

'Those four-valve heads were then used in various forms with various sizes of valve and port combinations on the slant six engines to give us early information.'

Thoughts then turned to producing an updated version of the venerable XK unit which could obviously be manufactured on existing facilities. Thus a four valve head was fitted to a 3.8 XK with redesigned block which was both easier to cast and lighter. Three such engines were built in 1976 with a bore of 90 mm and stroke of 100 mm. Both power output and fuel economy were satisfactory but it was considered that the engine still retained outdated features. For example, sealing the crank with a front lip seal housed half in the timing cover and half in the sump, and a rope seal at the rear had always been

a problem. Whilst it could be said that the Americans make satisfactory engines with these features, the production volumes which were now projected outstripped the capacity of the ageing XK tooling facilities.

A more major redesign was considered prudent and, moreover, whilst the engine just described might have been a suitable performer, it was felt that something considerably lighter would be needed as well. By this stage development work had commenced on the May high compression Fireball head for the V12 to improve consump-

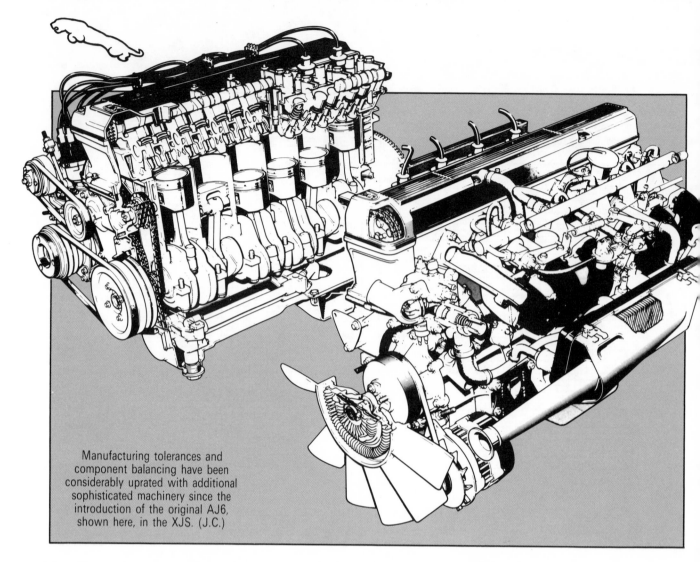

Manufacturing tolerances and component balancing have been considerably uprated with additional sophisticated machinery since the introduction of the original AJ6, shown here, in the XJS. (J.C.)

tion. The results were so encouraging that it was logically decided that the economy engine must have a similar head.

The decision was therefore taken to design a completely new six cylinder engine to be manufactured on a new block line. In order that the new engine could be fitted with a May head, produced on the same line as the May head for the V12, the one major constraint was that it must have the same cylinder bore centres as the V12.

The May combustion chamber with its lean burn characteristics works on the following principles. As the piston rises near the top of the compression stroke, it tends to squeeze the mixture under the rest of the head. This forces the mixture along the guide channel inducing in the gas a tangential jet action so pushing it into the deep

recess under the exhaust valve. This, in turn, provokes a very strong swirling turbulence, which very effectively speeds up the burning of the otherwise slow-to-ignite lean mixture.

As weight was one of the major considerations with the new engine, christened AJ6 (advanced Jaguar six-cylinder), aluminium was chosen as the material for the block and all major castings. This material had been used successfully on the V12, though rather less successfully on a handful of racing XK engines in the sixties which probably suffered from lack of serious development.

'We saw no reason,' states Crisp, 'to use anything other than aluminium for the block, except the cost, of course, was significantly more; but neverthel-ess we felt that if we were going to make an engine that was lighter than

the XK, particularly with the four-valve head, there was no way we were going to achieve that unless we used alumi-nium for the block.'

At about this time, several 6.4-litre V12 engines were constructed using a longer stroke and packers to lift the cylinder heads. At least two of these engines were fitted to cars, and the performance was apparently most ex-citing – so much so that serious thought was given to possible produc-tion use.

Harry Mundy also designed an 84 mm five-speed gearbox capable of accepting any foreseeable engine tor-que. Several prototypes were made. 'Needless to say both a 6.4-litre engine and a five-speed 'box found their way into Harry's car,' says Bob Knight. 'I believe the 77 mm Rover gearbox has a strong similarity to Harry's work.'

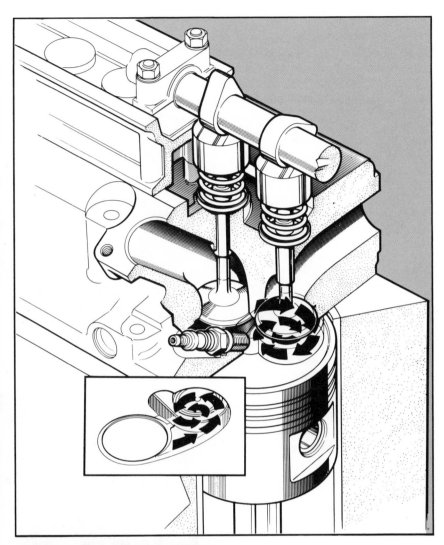

shrink-fit dry liners saving 3.8 kg. This course also had the added advantage of improving the torsional rigidity of the block, an important consideration for a possible diesel version. Indeed a deal of work has been done on diesel variants and such an engine is ready and waiting should it ever be needed.

During this period Mercedes introduced a V8 with pistons running direct in the aluminium bores and the alloy used for this purpose is known as a hypereutectic alloy.

At the end of 1979 Knight attended a BL Board meeting with Ray Horrocks and obtained the go-ahead for the AJ6 engine programme at a cost of about £32m. Knight was warned before going in that Ian MacGregor, more recently of British Steel and British Coal fame, being a metallurgist by profession and a member of the BL Board, was likely to try to ask technical metallurgical questions.

'When we got in there various people asked questions. MacGregor, when he considered the time was right said, 'Now Bob, have you considered the use of hypereutectic alloys on this engine?'

'That was a nice question and I could not have asked for a better one. Harry Mundy had been to the German foundry, who were producing the blocks for Mercedes, and they'd made comments on the design against the use of hypereutectic alloys, which Harry Mundy incorporated. My response to this effect at least made one friend on the Board!'

Trevor Crisp takes up the story again. 'At this time we made some 3.6, some 3.8 and we ended up with 3.6 more-or-less because at that time consumption seemed to be the major priority and we could get the performance we wanted out of a 3.6. The 2.9 was based on a Sales & Marketing requirement for something less than a 3-litre.'

The XJ40 project report produced by Engineering in 1981 yields the following information.

A total of 19 engines have now been built

The May combustion chamber, showing the induced swirl during the compression stroke. Inset is an underside view of the swirl pattern.

The original design for the AJ6 was Harry Mundy's before he retired and his work has been continued by Trevor Crisp, seen here. (J.C.)

Design work on the AJ6 began in 1976 and the first prototype ran early in 1979. These early engines had free standing iron liners, like the V12's, and the block was designed to be a die casting. Cost considerations, however, precluded this and a closed deck design was adopted using thin wall

of which 16 are 3.6 litre four-valve, two are 3.6 litre two-valve, and one is a 2.9 litre two-valve.

Four XJS cars are running with 3.6 litre four-valve engines, and an XJ6 with a 3.6 litre two-valve.

The total hours run on test bed engines is approximately 3000 hours of which 2000 is on four-valve engines. Total mileage is 12,000.

The major concentration of work has been on the four-valve engine as this is programmed to be in production one year earlier than the two-valve derivative and the major engine components other than cylinder head, are common to both designs. The two-valve cylinder head is virtually identical to the V12 design and consequently most of the proving on the XJ12 is directly relevant.

At this stage work was being concentrated on intake and exhaust manifold system optimization, noise reduction and lubrication system development. European emission tests had been performed and fuel consumption results gave 'Urban' figures of 16.1 mpg for the five-speed manual and of 16.5 mpg for the automatic.

Most two-valve development work was at this stage being carried out on the 3.6 and fuel consumption figures obtained by 'an XJ6 modified to simulate the weight and drag characteristics of the XJ40' amounted to 20 mpg for the 'Urban Cycle' and 42 mpg and 32.5 mpg at 56 and 75 mph, respectively.

The weight estimation of the 'four-valve' had been revised from 379 lb to 394 lb due to 'the use of additional balance weights on the crankshaft to improve engine refinement, and heavier than anticipated cylinder head castings'.

With regard to transmissions, it was originally intended to specify the Borg Warner Model 85 automatic transmission but that manufacturer decided to terminate development of this unit. Consequently Ford, ZF and GM transmissions were being considered and a GM item was being evaluated in an

XJS.

Concerning a manual 'box, the report stated, 'the Rover-Triumph 77 mm five-speed transmission is being specified although it is considered that the gearchange quality is not up to the standard expected from a high quality car in the XJ40 category. Development work is proceeding in conjunction with Land Rover to improve the 77 mm gearbox design'.

The 3.6 was launched in the XJS in October 1983 and immediately suffered an unfair comparison with the V12, which a six could obviously never match in terms of refinement. Intriguingly Jaguar were following their practice, first employed in 1948, when they chose to introduce the new XK engine first in a low volume sports car, the XK120, to prove the engine before launching the commercially more important Mark VII saloon range. Similarly the V12 was first available in the comparatively low volume Series III E-type. In this latest incidence of the practice it nearly backfired as direct comparison with the V12 could be made in the same body. Indeed there was much unfavourable comment.

There were some worries and Crisp with commendable candour admits this.

Undoubtedly refinement has been one of our biggest problems, some of which are attributable to the use of aluminium. Part of it is the shape of the block. The vee block does give you a more rigid structure than an in-line engine.

Most of our work has involved detail refinement in terms of tolerances on components and assembly balance, and the running clearance on pistons and bearings. These factors were not as critical on the XK engine with its lower maximum speed and

> The new 3.6 is not only a glamorous engine in the manner of its distinguished predecessor, it is also, like the XK in 1948, a most sophisticated one, being the only all-aluminium six in production in the world and having the very latest electronic wizardry. (J.C.)

the weight of its iron block helped to attenuate vibrations.

All the reciprocating components are now balanced to something in the order of half the tolerances we had on the XK engine. That's made a big difference.

The other big area where we've made things quieter is the cylinder head, particularly on the four-valve version. That was noisy initially, mainly due to the extra loads that you are imposing on the camshaft just by virtue of opening two valves at the same time instead of one. So you have a greater torque fluctuation as you turn the camshaft with the four-valve. We have made changes to the cam profile to smooth it out and made the valve gear lighter and the camshaft stiffer. The control of the timing chain has been improved and changes to the piston skirt design have reduced noise from this area.

Other changes include the adoption of lighter, thinner wall bucket tappets made of squeeze cast steel rather than cast iron and a redesigned crankshaft damper. Jim Randle admits that Jaguar's first objective was to build a reliable engine and refinement had, for once, taken a back seat. The development work has, however, saved the day and the early critics are now praising the engine installed in the '40'.

Two different engine management systems have been chosen. The 2.9 uses a Bosch LH Jetronic electronic injection and separate Bosch EZ-F programmed electronic ignition. The 3.6-litre is fitted with a newly developed Lucas combined micro-processor controlled ignition and injection system. One suspects that Jaguar have shrewdly chosen two manufacturers so as not to rely on a single source but also to be able to enjoy any future technological developments of either company.

The Lucas ignition and injection systems are combined into a common digital engine management system with their control units (ECU) integrated into one unit. The ignition is timed according to a 256 point map in its memory and takes signals from engine

sensors of throttle opening, crankshaft position, coolant temperature (air inlet temperature on US models) and engine speed. With such thorough control, it is able to time the sparks closer to the ideal advance curve for economy and efficiency.

Control of the fuel injection is centred round a by-pass hot-wire airflow meter. The mass of the air flowing into the engine is gauged by measuring the extra current needed to keep an electrically heated wire at a constant temperature when it is being cooled by the flow of air past it. Because such a method is affected by air density as well as air speed, it will automatically take account of the effects of changes in barometric pressure, such as when driving in mountainous country.

The 4 kilobyte memory ECU makes possible a number of rather clever features. For example, automatically maintained idle speed control compensates immediately for changes in load on an idling engine caused by operating such items as lights, fans or air conditioning.

A particularly novel feature of the Lucas system is its 'limp-home' ability. If any of eight different types of failure occurs the Vehicle Condition Monitor informs the pilot by displaying 'Fuelling failure'. A number is then displayed which later tells the mechanic precisely what has failed. The system then reverts to pre-set parameters stored in its memory to enable the car still to be driven to the nearest garage or wherever. As Crisp explains:

If for instance the airflow meter gives up the ghost, suppose somebody breaks the hot-wire, or somebody inadvertently pulls a connection off, then the system can recognise either that it isn't getting a signal at all or the signal is outside a certain span of operation. So the system will know that it isn't functioning correctly. Once it knows that it then substitutes a value in place of the air meter that will be at least sufficiently good to enable you to drive the car.

In the case of the air flow meter it will

give a signal that is just proportional to the throttle opening. So although it isn't a very accurate control of fuel, a driver probably wouldn't even pick it up. You could literally just pull off a connection and unless you were very sensitive I doubt whether you would know it wasn't working.

I enquired of Trevor Crisp whether emission control was still a problem.

It is, because all countries insist on having their own regulations. We have to keep making the decision, all the time, how many countries you lump together with one system. Is it worth having a dedicated system for a particular market? Catalysts are very expensive and if you can knock off half the volume of a catalyst you save hundreds of pounds. They are also detrimental to fuel consumption.

Sales & Marketing consider fuel consumption is still an important and sensitive area. In the States it is not just a matter of whether the customer is bothered or not because the authorities impose a tax on thirsty cars. In the past this has cost Jaguar Cars millions of dollars.

There are two different penalties. There is what they call a Gas Guzzler Tax which means you have to pay on a sliding scale if you are below 22$\frac{1}{2}$ mpg measured according to their test procedure. We do expect the XJ40 to be outside that but in addition to that there is what they call their Corporate Average Fuel Consumption and you have to better 27$\frac{1}{2}$ mpg for the average of your model range. There is no way any manufacturer who only produces large cars can meet that.

The 2.9 is a more economical engine more in terms of manufacturing cost rather than consumption. It is significantly cheaper to produce with the simpler head but less power dictates a lower axle ratio to maintain performance at a reasonable level and reduces the expected gain in fuel consumption.

As to the automatic transmission decided upon,

We wanted a four-speed automatic transmission and looked at a number of alternatives. At that time Borg Warner intended to produce a four-speed so we started off with them but they dropped their project and so we were left looking at GM, ZF and Ford. We plumped for ZF in the end though we did a lot of work with GM.

Interestingly Crisp mentions that Jaguar specified a number of changes to the ZF box and the Getrag manual 'box to achieve the desired levels of reliability. 'We have modified the overdrive gear set on the ZF to make sure that it would run continuously at maximum speed. There was a slight lack of lubrication previously.

Intriguingly, any modifications developed by Jaguar and incorporated by the manufacturers are being enjoyed by other users of the same products, including competitors!

As to credit for the design of the AJ6 engine, Crisp had this to say. 'Everyone deserves credit, but the original engine design was Harry Mundy's. We have developed it, installed it and got it into production.'

Mention of production brings us to Derek Waelend, the Manufacturing Director.

We have had to learn some unbelievable lessons about trying to make a refined all-aluminium engine. The XK engine could literally suffer out-of-balances on crankshafts and things of quite enormous amounts without having any effect on the engine because it was built like . . . one of those brick toilets!

We have learnt either through Southampton University or through IRD or through Schenk, who are balancing experts in Germany, some very hard lessons. For Manufacturing it's been quite dramatic because it all meant tightened tolerances. Where we were working to 50 gm/cm, we immediately halved it to 25. With the advent of all our new balancing machines, we are actually achieving 12 to 15, which is quite phenomenal. We have now got some very refined engines.

As to the future, Jaguar are currently playing with turbocharging and supercharging amongst other developments. There is a turbocharged 4-litre AJ6 on the stocks but it is my guess that the current vogue for adding turbos will diminish with such engines fading from the Grand Prix scene over the next couple of years.

Like the XK before it, there is plenty of room for development of the AJ6 with the future F-type and other projects to come. If we are not beset by another fuel crisis, my tip would be for some exciting V12 developments. Under-bonnet space probably precludes a revival of the 48-valve engine, but the 6.4-litre version which Mundy always wanted to produce, is, by all accounts, a phenomenal unit. Could it be Jaguar's answer to BMW and Mercedes?

Chapter 6
Craftsmen & Robots

Manufacturing was clearly an area for concern at Jaguar in terms of efficiency and productivity, which effectively means cost, and in terms of quality, which effectively means customer satisfaction. Starved of capital the plants remained antiquated or, where money had been invested in such areas as paint, it had proved less than satisfactory. But how much can a Jaguar plant be automated? As the industry hires more and more robots, is it possible for a company such as Jaguar, which still employs craftsmen and their skills, to hand-make a motor car in the more traditional way, to benefit from such modern technology without losing the inherent Jaguar qualities?

Mike Beasley, formerly Director of Manufacturing and now Assistant Managing Director, has played a large part in re-organising the three plants and improving standards. A production engineer by background, he joined Jaguar first in 1974 but after twelve to eighteen months and the publication of the infamous Ryder Report he moved to BL Cowley. The year 1979 saw him

back in the Jaguar fold, as Browns Lane Plant Director, just a few months before Egan joined. They have worked closely together since.

Not surprisingly Beasley has been heavily involved with the introduction of the XJ40.

My interest has been in trying to plan for its manufacture and to try and achieve a position where we can manufacture the car more easily, more readily with more integrity yet retain the 'Jaguarness' of the car when it is a completed article.

So we have tried to plan into the car new technology, better manufacturing methods, particularly in areas where we can get quality integrity as a result, and yet retain the essence of Jaguar with hand-cut leather, wood veneer selection, and that sort of thing.

When pressed to be more specific, Beasley has this to say.

I take the view that people stopped believing that the best idea was to hand scrape car engine bearings a long time ago.

Following spells with Ford, Jaguar, BL and Jaguar again, Mike Beasley was appointed a Plant Director in 1977, Manufacturing Director in 1980 and is today Assistant Managing Director. (J.C.)

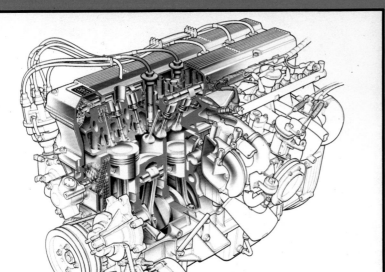

The 3.6-litre twin overhead cam all aluminium engine is fitted with a 24-valve head benefitting from the experience gained by Wally Hassan and Mundy at Coventry Climax during their era of designing and building highly successful Grand Prix engines. (J.C.)

Unfortunately there is no longer a British-manufactured automatic transmission suitable for Jaguar's use and so the company has been forced to look to the land of its rivals for this ZF unit. (J.C.)

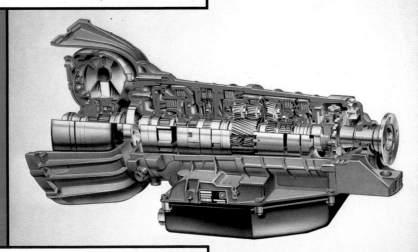

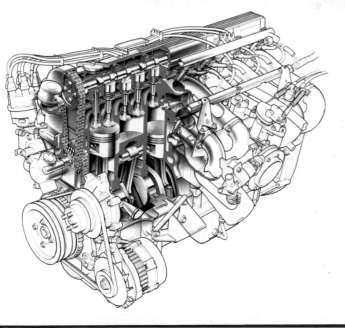

The 2.9-litre AJ6 employs a single overhead cam head that is very similar to the HE V12 engine which incorporates the principles devised by Swiss engineer, Michael May, and which was developed by Jaguar. (J.C.)

STUART SPENCER '85

1986
Jaguar Sovereign
Five Seater Saloon
Jaguar 6-cylinder · 3590cc · dohc · 4 v p c · 230 bhp · ca 221 km/h

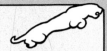

Stuart Spencer's cutaway illustration shows more clearly than could any photograph the 'inside' story of Jaguars new masterpiece. (J.C.)

JAGUAR

Jaguar's philosophy of providing a car which combines the traditional embellishments with unequalled modernity in engineering terms is reflected nicely in these two photographs, one of a craftsman veneer layer in the sawmill, and one of a production robot at the Castle Bromwich body plant. (J.C.)

Here at a styling clinic at Dusseldorf in October 1985, we see an example of the proposed new Jaguar and a variety of the new car's European competitors including, in the foreground, the car that was the hardest to beat, the Series III. (J.C.)

It is not just the exterior style that is judged at a clinic; an interior 'buck' is used to assess people's reactions to the seating, dashboard layout and so on. (J.C.)

The interior was to have been all plastic but thankfully as can be seen from this shot of a new XJ6, a certain amount of wood has been retained. (J.C.)

The most sumptuous interior is, of course, the Daimler with full leather trimming, heated seats, a distinctive, deeper and walnut veneered fascia. (J.C.)

The instrument panel includes electronic speedometer and tachometer in the centre, vacuum fluorescent gauges to the left with light switches below, whilst on the right are situated the dot matrix display and message centre below which are the controls for the trip computer. (J.C.)

The Jaguar Sovereign, with single headlamp treatment. (F. John French Agency)

The use of high contrast red lenses assist the rear styling and work on a similar principle to those at the front and side, allowing the tail lights, indicators and reversing lamps to shine through when in use, but providing a uniform colour theme the rest of the time. (J.C.)

The Jaguar Diagnostic System (JDS), which consists of a microcomputer and disc drive linked to a visual display unit, a printer and a keypad, uses probes to check current and measurement and can be fitted with additional 'pods' for fault finding on systems such as engine management and air conditioning. (J.C.)

I think there is a general appreciation that if you can apply, in machining areas for example, or in body-in-white construction, or in painting cars, manufacturing technology to improve quality and achieve more consistency, it will result in more integrity, therefore, in the build. So wherever possible we have gone that way with XJ40.

We needed to improve our facilities anyway having suffered from a long period of neglect in terms of capital investment in Jaguar and we had a lot of catching up to do. So we had the opportunity to catch up and bring in the latest, or close to the latest, levels of technology. The levels, that is, which were proven to be effective, which had a track record which we could see elsewhere.

We have introduced those into the Radford machining facilities, into the body construction, and we have even further moves in that area under way now, and in the painting. On the other hand the essence of a Jaguar is that you keep leather and it is hand-cut, and you use craftsmanship where a customer is seeing and touching the car. So we have retained that technique in those areas.

We tend to work with universities and suppliers. We've got a technology centre which comprises just a few specialists and their principal resources are outside with universities, both local and national. It is all aimed at getting more quality integrity into the parts and the build of the car.

In October 1983, Jaguar signed a collaborative agreement with Dainichi Sykes Robotics to jointly research AAMT, Advanced Automated Manufacturing Technology.

We didn't have any robots in Jaguar up until four years ago. Robots are not the panacea to all manufacturing problems by a long way, they just happen to be useful and industrious moving arms and they can do things consistently.

Dainichi Sykes had a good approach to a problem we put around the industry. The problem was polishing ports on the six and twelve-cylinder engines, blending the port from the machine surface of the valve seat through to the casting of the manifold. We

An early stage of the body-building process is the welding of chassis legs and front bulkhead panels in this jig. All welding stations are linked to a central control room where operations are monitored to ensure that welding standards are maintained. (J.C.)

The main floor is loaded into a four-post piercing fixture and after piercing is taken through various jigs where a number of brackets, crossmembers and sub-assemblies are fitted. (J.C.)

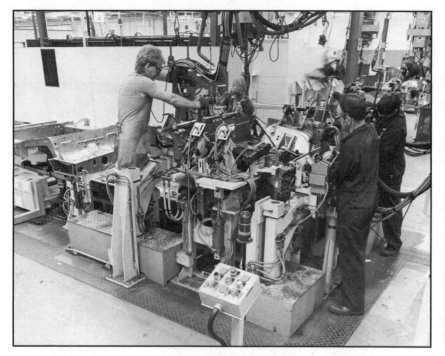

Above: Most resistance welding operations are carried out using portable gun stations at Castle Bromwich where some £10m has been invested in new body-in-white facilities (J.C.)

Below: The bulkhead, dash and bonnet hinge platform are joined to the main floor before the underbody passes on to an inspection fixture, where it can be rotated through 360 degrees enabling inspectors to check both sides. (J.C.)

used to do that by hand – lot of people and very mundane and mucky job – and we had the idea that we could have a robot to do it. But what we were looking for was a fairly advanced and sophisticated touch robot so that we could feel where the metal was or wasn't on the casting and where it was or wasn't on the machining and blend the two. Theoretically there are some fairly high tech solutions to that but Dainichi Sykes came up with a very practical solution which used the stiffness of a rubber block

to establish where the cutting tool went relative to the parts.

It works very well and as a result of that very practical and down-to-earth approach on application of robots, we signed an agreement which said we'd work together, with them as an extension of Jaguar's manufacturing engineering people. We've got quite a lot of projects underway and installed where we've used their engineers and ours jointly to solve problems.

Dainichi Sykes are not used exclusively. It is a matter of going to specialists in a particular field. Consequently Comau, who are acknowledged as amongst the finest line builders in the world, is being employed in manufacturing body sides at Castle Bromwich. The process is being extended to the whole of the body-in-white build.

More and more of the body will be built by flexible automation, though not necessarily by robots because they are not the only type of flexible automation. This is wholly, and in some instances solely, to achieve quality integrity. If they make a mistake, it is regular. If you can sort out the mistake, it's then consistently good. You can achieve perfection.

There are areas where you want human ingenuity and human consideration and we

After the building and fitting, by 10 robots, of the monosides, the application of sealant, and the fitting of front and rear screen frames and the roof, the flanges are dressed by a new machine which squeezes the flanges to produce the flat surface essential for sealing the windscreen, back lights and door apertures. (J.C.)

After passing the inspection in the joint and buy-offs sections, the bodies pass to the body build lines where bolt-on items such as bootlid, bonnet, front and rear doors, and bumpers are fitted. (J.C.)

plan that into the build of the car.

At present little has been done to automate engine assembly or final assembly of the vehicle. Technology is not there yet. 'The thinking robot has not arrived yet, nor are cars designed for that degree of flexible automation. We are looking at it on engine

After further inspection, during which inspectors wipe the bodies with a highlight fluid in an area fitted with high intensity lighting, the bodies are thoroughly washed with demineralised water and dipped for corrosion protection. (J.C.)

assembly and we've got one or two interesting notions.'

The relatively low volumes, high complexity of the cars and the model and market variations produced all mitigate against automation of final assembly and little change is foreseen here.

The other area that we've gone very heavily towards for XJ40, again with quality as the prime objective, is to shift off the idea that one does something, makes something and then someone inspects it, to the notion that you have a much higher degree of integrity in what you do if you consider what you are doing whilst you are doing it. The end product is bound to be right if every little element is right, as a philosophy. Whilst it is not a new technique, the computer allows it to be used more effectively. We've embraced the Statistical Process Control

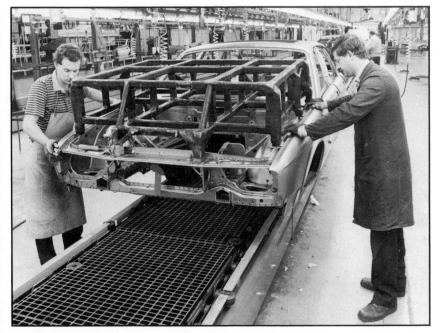

notion to ensure that we process capability, i.e. the process will perform and will achieve what we are asking of it and we are checking it at every stage of the way to know that it will achieve, and monitoring it on a regular basis. The end result is bound to be good.

Bearing in mind that many of Jaguar's quality problems have come from suppliers I enquired how this area had been tackled.

Again we have encouraged our suppliers to embrace the notion of Statistical Process Control. At the engineering end we have very closely specified what we want. We have specified the test routines and the environment in which the parts will be used.

We have a procedure, which we call MP17, in Jaguar where Engineering clearly specifies what we want. We then work with the supplier to understand what we want and agree it and accept it and sign it off before he even starts making it. Then we have a joint way of measuring how well he is doing, and whether or not his final result achieves the specification we set out to achieve in the first place.

Colin Johnson has the title of Project Engineer – SPC Department.

Not everybody can say 'statistical process control', so for short we call ourselves 'sausage, peas and chips' and everybody knows who we are then!

We have what are called 'process controlled robots' for measuring. This sort of equipment is capable of checking a car body with 900 points, that's probably 250 dimensions, in approximately six minutes. We, at Jaguar, have provided gauging with built in statistical control and given it, virtually, to the suppliers to ensure that they do meet the standards that we expect. We have got quite a nice system running with three major suppliers producing cross beams and rear frame items, which are safety-critical items, whereby they can't send us bad parts. Each one is stamped. If it's not stamped, it's not a good one and they also have to send us a cassette tape of

No less than £15m has been expended on new 'clear over base' paint technology, completed in June 1986, and following baking and curing, all enclosed box sections and structural areas are flooded with hot wax. (J.C.)

all the dimensions for that batch. The tape is run and if there is anything wrong, the whole batch is rejected.

At the moment it's hard work; but who cares about hard work? We're enjoying it all.

Whilst Mike Beasley's responsibilities now lie in overall manufacturing strategy, Derek Waelend is responsible for production and the day to day running of the three plants. The two

gentleman could not be more different in manner. Beasley is a quietly spoken man who chooses his words carefully whereas Waelend is a fast talking, ebullient cockney character. Both inspire tremendous confidence in the future of Jaguar.

Ken Edwards, Director and Company Secretary, is in charge of Personnel and clearly remembers he and Beasley interviewing Waelend. They had him in mind as a Plant Director but both agreed that here was an ideal man to be XJ40 Project Director. This he became.

When I arrived to see him, he explained courteously that we would have to make another appointment because he was short of time but he would just cover a few points. His

Completed body shells are then stacked automatically in the body store at Castle Bromwich, before being plucked by computer-controlled handling machinery in the order required on the assembly tracks at Browns Lane. (J.C.)

infectious enthusiasm for his job obviously got the better of him because I left his office nearly two hours later!

Waelend joined Jaguar in early 1983 after 23 years with Ford. He has always been involved in manufacturing having been associated with quality, manufacturing engineering, maintenance, and production at various European plants plus development and manufacturing development, and with the introduction of several new models. Jaguar had not introduced a new model since the XJ-S in 1975 and a completely new model since the original XJ6 in 1968, and so were lacking in this area of experience.

*I was asked, because the project was in a pretty poor state, to take over the direc-*torship of the XJ40 project. So I said immediately, 'yes', not really understanding what I was letting myself in for and that was quite clear in a very short period of time – like the next day when I was in the boardroom having to give a progress report!

But since then I've spent three years doing nothing else but living, eating, drinking, sleeping XJ40. I was the leg that took the design from Jim Randle and put it into production. I was the sort of intermediate leg and that has allowed me to paddle about in both ponds. That has had a fantastic advantage for me, a good advantage for the product and also for Engineering.

Very early on we laid down certain specific requirements, and one of those requirements was that most, if not all, of Jim's development cars would actually be built by Manufacturing. Other than the first five or six cars which were hand put together, all the remaining ones were built

in separate facilities. I have now built [August, 1986] over 350 cars of which 250 odd, in some form or another, have gone towards the development of this car, whether it's in training or service or for Jim Randle himself.

Phasing a new car into production can be a difficult and testing time for a motor manufacturer.

We are basically a one model company, we could never live on XJ-S alone. With my last company it was never a problem, you could shut down one line, you could turn another plant up, you could turn the other models up, and then you brought in the new car and you didn't even see the hiccups. But here if we bring in a new model and stop, we die.

We had to do it in separate facilities. So we took the opportunity to build brand new body-in-white facilities in a completely refurbished block that used to make Minis down at Castle Bromwich. At Radford we had already put in brand new facilities for the AJ6 engine which we introduced in the XJ-S, and very wisely so because there were a lot of refinement problems which we've now sorted out.

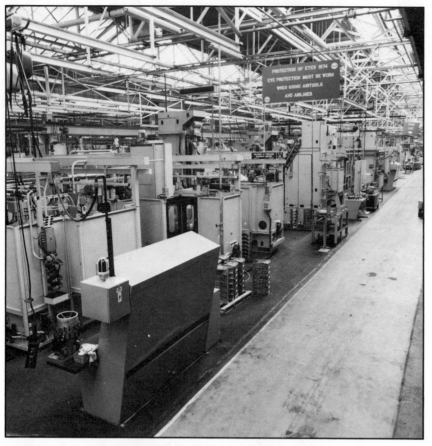

Here at Browns Lane, we were faced with more serious problems because the only way to introduce the new car was to actually build it down our tracks and I only have three tracks here, two for the saloons and one for the XJ-S. So we decided we needed a separate build facility and we turned an old paintshop here, by investing just over half a million, into a pilot plant facility. It is probably the best decision Jaguar's ever made and the best money they have ever spent.

It has enabled me to work in total isolation without interrupting the current production of Series III. The pilot plant facility is a small version of the main assembly tracks. It represents all the same problems, it is built the same way, has the same pillars, stanchions, etc., and we can simulate the main lines. It has been invaluable.

Secondly, because of the facility I could manufacture all the cars and that meant I got involved very early. That had two advantages. It meant that I could stamp my requirements, that is Manufacturing's re-quirements, on the car and secondly it meant that Jim Randle got better built cars. If you put a car together in the development shop, you're never quite sure whether a bloke's fettled a little bit to make it fit. Whereas using normal operators they will say, 'can't fit this, can't fit that'. It is much more realistic.

I think even Jim would now admit that it has been a valuable asset to Engineering. I used to be a pain in the arse to them because I used to say, 'Hang on Jim, I don't want that, I want this because it is easier to put in'. So I have been able to

stamp a lot of manufacturing requirements very early on in the product.

It has grown the two departments much closer together.

Also being the Project Director and having total responsibility to the Board, I had nobody working for me because I kept very lean. It basically meant that I could go and concentrate where I saw problems. One of the areas where that was very relevant was in engineering changes. I am the ultimate authority for engineering changes.

Engineering were not happy with that at times. I think they thought, 'Why should this rough-neck production man be allowed to over-rule us?'

At the beginning of 1986 Mike Beasley

was made Assistant Managing Director to relieve Sir John Egan of some of his workload and Waelend stepped up to take Beasley's job. Having been thoroughly immersed in XJ40, he moved to being responsible for the manufacture. He is, therefore, now in charge of the three plants.

Several months before the launch the pilot line was running at a progressively increasing rate, on day shift only, producing most of the launch stock, plus cars required by Engineering, the Press cars, homologation cars, photographic cars and so on.

We made those cars in specific phases. We started with phase one and ended with phase eight. At the end of each phase there was a specific requirement for those cars and each time I used to attempt to raise the standard from the previous phase. So we got to phase seven and I said 'Right, this must be to a mechanically saleable standard, but cosmetics we'll still work on'. So we got to phase eight and they had to be

mechanically and cosmetically saleable, and that put early pressure on to the organisation.

We took three of the cars and subjected them to total company audit, involving every department. We came up with a list of 260 items on the car that we didn't like. Some were serious concerns, others were trivia. I was tasked by the Chairman to get all those fixed in six weeks. That's a gigantic task.

With my cavalier attitude we got every supplier in, with Purchase, and said to the supplier, 'That's the problem. I want it fixed. Worry about drawings after'. For example, the gasket for the mirror had a point and the mirror had a radius, doesn't look nice. So I said, 'There's a mirror. Make the gasket fit that. Goodnight. Right next person.' It was a madhouse – but it worked.

It was in fact all done under control because I had alongside me a design engineer, a process engineer and the purchase man and as I spoke to the suppliers they were writing out a notification to engineering of the change. We

have now got all but a handful of those fixed and introduced on to the pilot build. It was a mammoth undertaking and all our suppliers and engineering people have to be complimented for achieving this task in such a short time.

I have a marvellous area called Assembly Development which is a satellite area between Engineering and Production. Anything that is released from Engineering for Production is checked before it's introduced on the track by Assembly Development. They do the initial proving and they are very skilled track fitters with years of experience and they really come up with an enormous amount of quick fixes. A lot of these problems were solved by them.

Engineering have now accepted that. Whereas before a designer had to design something on paper, give it to Purchase to go and buy, and then I got the first sample and said, 'Oh! dear, oh! dear, it doesn't work'. We now have a situation where most designers go down there and say, 'I am thinking of doing this'. They discuss it and can actually make a sample because they can do almost anything down there. They have access to vac-forming facilities, the woodmill, painting facilities, trim shop, electrical areas, etc.

It also happens to be the area where we do all our police cars, all our high security vehicles and all the special requirement vehicles for VIPs.

Waelend is concerned that with the Engineering and Styling Departments moving to the separate plant at Whitley communication and the rapport will suffice.

We are trying to overcome that by ensuring that at Whitley they have a pilot facility and my people will be there building the cars. So I will have very early knowledge of the new cars. We will make all the cars up to the pilot build stage there then we'll transfer them here to my pilot plant, run an initial batch down here and then onto the main lines.

When I came to the company, we were going to have a worldwide launch, which was absolutely suicidal. The logistics of trying to launch in all markets on the same

day and the problems for manufacturing would have been horrendous.

At that time we were still under the BL umbrella and they could not conceive that the car could take six years. They said we'd got to get it out in four and a half. So really, in some instances, we were playing games in telling them when the car was coming out, knowing the actual time. No-one can get a car out, no matter who they are, as complicated as ours, inside six years, and we are just about there.

The problem was that we had to kid everybody it was coming out in 1984 and that has had a very bad effect on a lot of our suppliers. AB Electronics, for example, have had a 50,000 square foot factory sitting there for two years. They also had the Sinclair C5 – not, probably, two of their greatest commercial decisions!

We've had so many false starts. One of the problems has been only being able to let the leash out a little at a time, so each time we've said the project's going back six months when we really knew it was two years. If we'd told everybody it was going to be two years, I think it would have been better but I think there was always the concern that if engineers are given the time they will fill it with more development rather than fixing the problems we wanted fixed.

I wanted a year's split between the UK and States launches but they said that was too long, the Series III would go down the pan. So we have now decided on six months. Therefore I am building for the UK at the moment and I am building in batches, my highest volume first. It is all Sovereigns at the moment. I will build several hundreds of those, get plenty of experience then introduce XJ6, which is down spec slightly – different instruments, lights, black door frames instead of chrome, etc. Then we go to Daimler next and they are quite significantly different.

So as soon as I have done that for the UK then I introduce France, which has, for instance yellow headlamps, that sort of thing. Then we go to Italy, Belgium, Switzerland, Australia, Middle East, Japan and right at the very end I'll introduce Federal [US] market.

By that time we will have had feedback

from UK customers and be able to introduce quick fixes on problems that they have found that we haven't found. There are bound to be some. We must get everything fixed before we go to the States because the States is really our home market. It take 55 per cent of my volume and gives us 75 per cent of our revenue. So I cannot play games with that.

Derek Waelend claims that the company has achieved every objective they have set themselves with regard to time. The time every phase started and finished has always been met though sometimes it has been,

the twelfth hour of the last day – and that's a great thing. Jaguar has never achieved timing and objectives on the introduction of a new model before.

In amongst all this we said we will never, ever, ever launch a new car and a new paint system at the same time. We've done it!

The last time we changed our paint

Derek Waelend is a most likeable man of considerable energy. Having been at Ford for 23 years, he took charge of the XJ40 project and his dynamic efforts have been rewarded by promotion to Manufacturing Director. (J.C.)

technology, which was in 1980 I think, it was a disaster, it almost crippled the company. We would only sell yellow, white and red cars and it was a terrible situation. We've changed our paint technology again and that's been very dramatic from a production point of view.

The changeover went very well and we were up and running very quickly. We are under 10 per cent first time reject rate, which is phenomenal. We went to Mercedes, ourselves, and they were having nearly a 40 per cent reject rate first time.

We electro-coat the car, then we put primer on, we wet sand that all over, then we put a surfacer coat on, then a sealer, followed by an orange guide coat. We then oil sand that lot all over until the orange coat disappears and we know then that we have got rid of all the blemishes but we haven't taken too much off. We use a scientific measurement by using a meter to measure gloss/reflectively. We are getting reflective rates now that are far superior to our competition. We use a scale of ten, a perfect mirror being ten, and we are up near the tens.

The new paint system works as follows. Paint is forced out of an orifice on to the back of a bell spinning at around 30,000 rpm. This atomises the paint which is also electrostatically charged and together with a downdraught in the booth the paint mists down to the body and is drawn to all surfaces of the shell, inside and out.

Developments at Radford with regard to engine manufacture I have covered in Chapter 5, but Waelend also mentioned that the new axles are much easier to build than Series III. He also stressed the tolerances now being worked to on the brake discs.

The actual machining tolerances are quite phenomenal. We are talking about tenths of a thou. We don't have any more than three tenths of a thou runout in every 50 degrees. We have all new machines to do that because if you are talking about tenths, your machines have to be capable of working to a tenth of that.

Here at Browns Lane we are still assembling on tracks that once assembled the Triumph Mayflower which Sir William had bought secondhand from Standard Triumph. I want to get to some high tech tracks with suspended assembly with the doors off because open doors means problems. We have developed some lift-off hinges. With just one bolt we can lift the door off and put it back on again.

We can then assemble the doors away from the tracks. Also I want the suspended carriers to be able to tilt the body through 90 degrees, so that the jobs that are at present done from the pit, can then be worked facing you. You can bring the engines round on an AGV, an automatic guided vehicle, and fit them from below. So those are the sort of plans we have in mind.

We have problems with our unique situation of a lack of model ranges. But with what Jim Randle and Geof Lawson have in the pipeline for us, I'm going to need more space because we are going to get a nice spread of models like Sir William used to have. It is necessary so that you can play tunes with production and maximise efficiency and more easily introduce new models.

Waelend, in spite of his high volume orientated background, is adamant that traditional Jaguar qualities must remain. He waxes lyrical about the Daimler specification. Referring to this he says, 'There are sixteen pieces of wood in the car and it is one hundred per cent leather! We have the largest trim shop in Europe with over a thousand people'.

He roared with laughter when I pointed out that here was a Ford man who was anti plastic interiors and extolling traditional virtues. 'We are selling an executive car to very exclusive customers. They expect it. I can change my hat, but my fanatical insistence is that I want to get Jaguar to the build consistency of the high volume manufacturers. When you are making 2,000 cars a day like Volkswagen you have got to have absolute build consistency. I want that with all the natural traditions of Jaguar expertise in materials and design. We must merge the two together. That's how we've got to grow.'

To many people's relief, and none more so than the men involved, the craftsmen still have an important part to play alongside all the new high technology. Terry Williams, with 33 years service, is one of the skilled craftsmen who produce the veneered trim that distinguishes a Jaguar from its foreign competition. He explained a few aspects of the process to me.

The veneer starts life in California as a walnut tree which would have been planted eighty to a hundred years ago. The bit we are really most interested in is the bole under the ground. To be cut it then travels to France, Italy, Germany or Switzerland and we receive a veneer of half a millimetre thickness. We actually send agents abroad to search for this veneer for us – it isn't quite like buying sausages or sweets!

We work on a log system for our cars because we depend upon a matching car set. Other manufacturers will be happy with cutting a strip of veneer ignoring the fact that one side of a car will be a totally different colour to the other side of the car. At Jaguar we insist on a system where we use one log, because that log will be the only one of that colour and we'll only produce a matching set from that log. On top of that, the veneers form a mirror image across the centre-line of the car.

It used to be traditional that we laid our veneers on mahogany wherever possible. Nowadays with the weight constraints upon a car, we have to use other materials and use a laminating process to a large extent. We take best quality Finnish birch plywood, which is about the best quality in the world we can get, and the most stable, and laminate on the front with a 4 mm very dense mahogany veneer and on the back we laminate another mahogany veneer, lay it in our bag press on a former on a curve and then machine that section. We are then happy that there is a stable surface for us to lay our walnut veneer on.

For reasons of thickness or strength, there are some sections we can't make in wood and they have to be steel. So we

have had to design systems that enable us to lay veneers on steel successfully in large quantities. To do this we zinc plate the steel, degrease – we've found a primer it is possible to spray on – and then use a normal woodworking glue.

The inlays used on a Jaguar are a true boxwood, fixed in the traditional method by very accurately machining a groove slightly undersize. The boxwood, with the corners mitred, is then fixed by pushing in with glue and a hammer, and then planed or scraped off to the surface level of the veneer, and then sanded and finished.

The lacquer finish is sprayed on with a linear head which can read the distance it has to travel, control the coat we are putting on in grammes per square foot and, in fact, travels sixteen or eighteen feet for a natural flow to be achieved on the surface and then the item goes through ultra violet lamps. To achieve the required Jaguar standard of finish, we make three passes of that process, flatting by hand between each coat. The final finish is then linished by large mops, rotating in each direction, sprayed with a cutting paste.

Another area where craft skills are seen is the leather cutting department of the trim shop where fully cured and dyed hides are examined by the individual cutters to ensure grain match and avoid blemishes. Between two and four hides are used, depending on model, and all seats are hand sewn.

It is a startling thought that these two groups of craftsmen, and that term includes many women, are now producing in excess of 1,000 sets of veneered panels and trim per week.

Derek Waelend is a tremendously approachable person who radiates energy and drive. 'The labour force is dramatically changing. I go down the tracks, they see me, the Manufacturing Director. They know if they have a problem I can help them. This is a total change; they have never seen this before. Normally managers are aloof but I am not that kind of person. I try and treat all people the same because they are my greatest asset. We spend a tremendous amount of time and money

Inset: At Browns Lane is the largest trim shop in Europe. Skilled craftsmen still select up to four hides per car ensuring grain match and avoiding damaged areas, then cut the hides, hand sew and assemble all the seats. (J.C.)

Left: From the Browns Lane body store the bodies commence their journey down the assembly line with electrical items here being fitted to the front bulkhead. (J.C.)

performance, etc.'

Good communication is undoubtedly one of the most important aspects of business today. At Jaguar there is now much better communication between management and workforce, a state confirmed by Waelend:

I have never seen anything like the level of co-operation achieved through this project in my life before.

My philosophy now is, let's get the car on the road. Then we'll start taking some of

One of the big advantages the XJ40 has over the Series III is that it is designed so that the engine does not require fitting through the bonnet aperture . . .

. . . thus the body can be 'dropped', which is safer, simpler and less likely to damage paint, on to the entire power train, all of which has been built at Radford, thoroughly tested and transported to Browns Lane. (J.C. both)

keeping the workforce informed. Every Monday morning the foreman stands with his people and goes through a brief telling them about latest things like the racing results, quality, cost

the cost out by reducing the build hours. Our true competition is Mercedes and we have not been the best as far as durability

107

with Series III has been concerned. But '40' gives us that match. We've got a good car, an excellent car, a world class car!

The manufacturing process time on Series III is about 200 hours. On XJ40 it's less than 150 hours. That is a substantial improvement and it means that a quarter of my labour force is now available for higher volume. We've got to get better because, just consider that the Ford Granada, which I do not consider a competitor but for comparison's sake, is manufactured, without the power train side, in about 43 hours.

As more automation is introduced, it will release more labour to increase production in other areas with re-training.

But there will be no sacrifice whatsoever to the quality standards and vehicle refinement. That really is a traditional Jaguar feature that I think most other manufacturers would find it very difficult to match. Some are getting near but when XJ40 is launched, they will realise how much of a quantum leap we have gone ahead again. I think it's quite phenomenal.

Production by 1980 had slumped to

During assembly of further component parts, electrics, interior and exterior trim, the body panels are fitted with protective covers to safeguard the all-important paint finish – even the operators overalls are designed without damaging buckles, buttons and belts. (J.C.)

just 13,791 cars. It improved a little the following year to 14,577 and jumped in 1982 to 22,046. By 1983 the figure at 28,041 was looking more reminiscent of better times and the impressive trend continued in 1984 with 33,437 vehicles produced. A year later the volume was approaching 40,000 units. Jaguar, in fact, stated in 1983 that they intended to achieve a production figure of 60,000 by 1990, if not the late eighties. I asked Mike Beasley if that was realistic.

We have done a lot of work with our employees in terms of wanting to achieve security of employment. We want to achieve growth without adding too many people. We want to achieve growth through productivity which in the main is going to mean using new equipment to replace the old, new facilities and new

After passing along the track for completion of assembly, the car receives a major electrical check known as VETS – Vehicle Electrical Testing System. (J.C.)

technology.

Growth is going to come from doing more right first time, with better quality standards generating more sales, more volume being achieved through more productivity. That is the basic essence of the business. We are going for steady growth of ten or fifteen per cent per annum. A super position for a luxury car maker is to make one less car than he can sell.

Apart from selling more of each model, Jaguar aim to grow families from each model in order to satisfy a wider spread of the market place and give the company more security at the same time. 'I've got some interesting challenges,' states Beasley, 'over the next few years. Furthermore we have

Above: At the end of the track, the car is gas charged to check for leaks in the air conditioning system, is inspected, passed off for rolling test and taken for a 5 – 8 mile test run on local roads. (J.C.)

Below: With a final polish, and on this one, fitment of the grille and headlamp trim, the XJ6s, Sovereigns and Daimlers are ready for delivery to the dealers. (J.C.)

got to get more UK suppliers up to European standards.

Space is a problem at Browns Lane and, as mentioned, a new Engineering Department is being set up at Whitley. This means that the company will then be operating from four separate plants, which hardly seems a perfect situation.

Ideally it would be one site, but if it was it would be too big and unmanageable, and there are some instances of that around the country. Ours are a nice size and there is good identity within the plants.

I don't mind moving cast aluminium or cast iron around, it's nice solid stuff and the cost of moving it from Radford to Browns Lane is minimal. You would have to move it around a factory anyway so putting it on a truck for two miles is not important. Moving bodies around is not a good idea, shipping fresh air, which is what you are doing. We've minimised that as much as we are able by having a computer-controlled store at Castle Bromwich which is fed automatically from the paintshop and a computerised store at Browns Lane which feeds automatically to the main assembly. They are interlinked and the trucks that run between literally do plug in electronically to the computer stores and get filled automatically with the right schedule of bodies.

Over a five to six year period the company will be spending £80/100m per year split pretty evenly between the three main sites. As to the future, Beasley states that they are planning the next five years firmly and the next ten tentatively, throughout the whole business. As to the avowed intention of 60,000 cars by the end of the decade, 'we expect to achieve that comfortably'.

Chapter 7
Legend Reborn

Marketing consists of very much more than just selling cars although that is, of course, the ultimate aim. Equally a marketing department does not first become involved with selling the product when that product is first produced. There are many aspects to a modern marketing department including dealer promotions, advertising, sponsorship, new product development, business planning, franchise planning and so on. But it all starts with market research, something we have all heard of but very few of us actually know very much about.

At Jaguar this subject was for two years the preserve of Joe Greenwell who joined the company in 1983 as Marketing Research Manager. From this he has graduated to Product Strategy Manager, which he describes as being 'asked to put my money where my mouth is'. This involves defining closely the sort of product and features, and specification characteristics, for vehicles currently on the drawing board. Furthermore he is responsible for carrying through to launch the mar-

keting plans developed for the XJ40.

Having drawn up a marketing brief for the vehicle worldwide, his job has been to make that brief available to external agencies closely concerned with the launch.

Before 1983 Jaguar bought a marketing research service from BL. Following the establishment of a separate Sales and Marketing Dept in 1982, marketing research and volume planning were two further areas that were brought within Jaguar control.

In the late seventies/early eighties quite a lot of concept work was done assessing early consumer response to interior and external bucks of the '40' in the States and Britain. This early exploratory research led to product clinic tests. Apart from using clay and fibre-glass mock-ups for engineering and styling development work, these bucks can also be shown to specially selected customer groups to test their reaction. As Mike Beasley puts it, 'We have to be sure we've got what the customer wants. It is no good building even a super product if no-one wants

to buy it'.

Greenwell stresses the importance of obtaining reactions at a very early stage.

When you have signed off the body-in-white, you have more or less signed off the exterior styling. It was absolutely critical that the style of the new car generated a favourable response. We knew it was the key factor in generating the special magic and aura of Jaguar saloon ownership. The new car's style will establish worldwide how successful the car is likely to be at continuing the magic and evoking the aura of Jaguar saloons.

So it is a very, very important decision. Once that decision is made you are then into other no less important decisions involving the interior packaging. For that you need a fully working interior prototype that has a wheel, an instrument binnacle, an air con panel, door casings, everything. Some of those parts will be one piece mock-ups rather than off tools, but they are built to last the course for five or six day product tests be they in the States, Europe or over here.

Styling clinics have played a major part in the XJ40 project since its inception. (J.C.)

Clinic tests, sometimes known as Hall tests, are used by many consumer product companies including motor manufacturers. Greenwell explains:

What you are doing is putting your product in a controlled test against competitive products and, probably, some of your existing products to assess whether you are moving in the right direction.

Specifically, a car clinic involves a number of stages. The selection of a secure venue is an obvious need. You will choose anything from a hotel ballroom to a major air-conditioned or heated warehouse, preferably with no windows, preferably with only one entrance and all other entrances sealed or guarded. It is all quite glamorous stuff!

Venues have included Sandown Park rececourse, Effingham Park in Sussex, a major hotel in Dusseldorf and a major conference hall next to a theatre and leisure complex designed by Frank Lloyd Wright in San Francisco.

This was probably the best we have ever used because it was large, secure, well lit and well aired, and in the meat of our market place in terms of area. You need to pick a place that is going to be secure. We have teams of security guards who are selected by our own company protection officers here. If you are going to show a vehicle that is kitted up to look representative of showroom condition but you don't intend to make if for seven years, you can do without too much publicity!

You put your new vehicle alongside your existing vehicle and then as standard references a BMW '7' Series, a Mercedes 'S' Class, a Cadillac Seville, maybe, and you select, carefully recruit, 250/300 people. They qualify by dint of either owning one of your cars or one of your competitors' cars, or being likely to own one within the next four to five years. We

A clinic, such as this one at Sandown Park Racecourse in January 1984, can cost in the region of £75/100,000 to stage. (J.C.)

Styling clinics have been held in all Jaguar's major markets including the States where one was held at San Francisco in January 1986. (J.C.)

call them 'aspirants'. Those are the people on the up, the upwardly mobile groups who could be in your market in a very short time.

You submit those people to a process of self administered questionnaires concerning their basic demographics, their attitudes to driving and vehicles in general. This is so that with the more sophisticated types of analyses available today you can segment this little microcosm of a market place by dint of their attitudes rather than a simple, straightforward socio-economic grouping.

They go round and rate the car from the exterior and give a detailed appraisal of the interior covering the ergonomic and cosmetic aspects. After that they are probably interviewed by a trained interviewer probing away at the detail of their responses and others are likely to be involved in a group discussion which is quite often moderated by a consultant psychologist. The process can take anything from two and a half to eight hours, depending on how interested people are.

We generally find that with a Jaguar secure clinic the interest is very high

By January, 1986 all major styling decisions had obviously been taken but clinics were still used to check items of external trim, for example, which though subtle can still make an important contribution to style. (J.C.)

he would expect to find inside a Jaguar saloon. He is motivated to purchase by the qualities of traditionalism, crafted materials, leather, wood and chrome. These qualities are perceived as not present in many of the luxury domestic products emanating from Detroit.

A Jaguar is a brisk accelerator, is regarded as an extraordinarily comfortable car to drive, the ride/handling is unique and is generally a much sought after vehicle. A lot of our vehicles are sold in California, Florida and Long Island, New York. You will find a lot of women driving around in 380SLs and a lot in XJ-Ss. Women are very important indeed to us in the States. At the last count of the Jaguar Vanden Plas cars that we sold, 55 per cent of the principal

A US styling clinic, such as this one at San Francisco, can cost $1/4m but is considered cost-effective and essential to reduce the risks of non-acceptance. (J.C.)

indeed, response rates are very good and people take it very seriously and we get good information.

Not surprisingly the market and typical owners vary enormously from country to country.

Over here the typical XJ6 driver is probably a company director, gets his car through the company and the company judges that it is important that a man of that standing should drive that type of vehicle. In the States you very commonly find such a high level of personal and household wealth that they will sometimes run six and seven vehicles. A year ago the mean income was in excess of $125,000. About one in five is earning in excess of a $1/4m. The decision is, therefore, not such a critical one. It is a very different pattern of purchase, very prestige, status-orientated.

'The US customer tends to be generally more conservative in his attitudes to what

In the States only one domestic vehicle is included, as the usual imported rivals are perceived to be the main competition in that market as well. (J.C.)

drivers were women. They will select it, they will pick the colour and trim, and they will drive it. So it is important to include women in the consumer clinics.

American customers tend to value tradition, heritage, style and European panache. It is a means of demonstrating to the world that you are urbane, wordly wise and have taste.

Over there you find women using the cars to go to the country club, going shopping, living in a Dallas-type mode.

Over here the market is somewhat different. Jaguar ownership is a means of expressing, for the 45/50 year old man, to the world, that he has arrived or been around for some while and that he has achieved something. Because they are less

rare here, the demand for updating technological progress is perhaps greater here than over there.

Germany and the UK are probably less sensitive to the wood, chrome and leather than the United States. Over here we have to earn our corn competing against BMW's who have a more 'yuppie', sporty-type image; a younger age profile. We have to try to win business from there and also prove our worth on resale value grounds where Mercedes perform particularly well. So slightly different needs in the market place over here, though still the fundamentals are there – style, elegance, product quality, the 'grace, space and pace'.

If we are to sustain credibility with this new car in Europe, and in particular Germany, we cannot let ourselves down on product quality. Mercedes are rivalled only in terms of dependability and reliability by Honda and possibly Toyota – according to our information. Mercedes are extraordina-

rily good at staying together over stressful periods like long stretches on the autobahn at maximum speed. These are very trying conditions for any vehicle but if your domestic manufacturer can do it, then if we are going to take business away from that company in the quantities we hope to, we must match these standards.

The Australian importers carry out their own research which is fed back to Browns Lane. They also concentrate heavily on good communication with their dealers and customers, dealing direct with the latter if they are not achieving satisfaction from the former.

From market research a strategy is formed which dictates how the new car should be designed to sell. Some manufacturers who, perhaps, have a wide range of vehicles, can afford to be more adventurous and take risks that will not ultimately dictate their very

existence. Others, like Jaguar at present, depend on one model and the decisions are necessarily more momentous.

We have built a car that will continue to be instantly recognised for what it is, but be an obvious update as well. That is the marketing strategy. One doesn't want to walk away from an acknowledged strength. The sensible money goes on just a modest updating of an existing formula and style. That doesn't mean you have to be overcautious in terms of design or other aspects of the engineering achievement. There are whole areas of the car that are completely new – every panel, the engine, the spec's totally different, but it is good sound commercial practice not to go walking away from your centres of business and the reasons for your success which are style, elegance, prestige, the dynamic characteristics of the car and value for money.

There are a number of justifications for Jaguar's involvement in the world of motor sport such as fostering a sense of pride in the workforce. But what of the marketing benefits?

I think it is extremely important. It is clear that Jaguar's continuing involvement is a necessary condition for sustaining the sort of image we have and continuing to nourish it. I would not want to be part of a marketing department that was recommending against motor sport.

It supports what I think is the correct commercially aggressive policy, taking on the best and trying to beat them. That is where Jaguar should be every time. Just as it takes them on in world markets in terms of professionalism, it should take them on on every front it can.

As Greenwell stated, it is important for Jaguar to try to again capture the younger owner who has bought BMW's in recent years because they were considered trendy. Motor sport can only assist this image just as it did in the fifties and sixties when the Mark 2 saloons had the BMW market.

Pricing policy is another area of marketing strategy. Jaguar has tended towards less pricing spread since the introduction of the original XJ6 in 1968, and consequently narrowed its market. There are also considerations as to whether a company should charge for a large range of options or sell a comprehensive spec. Mercedes and BMW follow the former policy but Jaguar do not, preferring, as they put it, 'to be more generous'.

Jaguar has long had a reputation of offering the best for less than anyone else. Our general policy on XJ40 has tended to be to support our reputation for value for money. No-one does it better than us. We intend to price fairly aggressively in order to attract the up-and-coming young executives, the people who are driving Rover 800s, Saabs, Audis, Scorpios, Renault 25s. That's where John Morgan feels we were in the fifties and that's where he wants one part of us to be today.

John Morgan has been one of the pillars of Jaguar for many years having joined the company Export Dept. from Rootes in 1963.

The first thing we had to do was to rebuild the base for our car distribution throughout Europe. During the years of the BL franchise policy for Jaguar, we had lost a tremendous amount of image and were losing volume at an alarming rate in most countries, to the point that the BL director responsible for forward planning had said that we had virtually lost our base and there was certainly no future for the V12, there was no future for the 'S' and in fact there was no future for Jaguar.

So we were in a very parlous position in Europe, with a totally demoralised dealer organisation and the product itself we knew lacked a lot. I knew only too well because I had been in Japan only just before that and had to put up with a lot of the problems there. I had a lot of sympathy with the dealers.

We had to rebuild on the basis that Jaguar had to be taken out of this amorphous mess of makes which didn't

have any particular image and its image had to be rebuilt. That took us a number of years but it was based entirely on one thing. Namely, to reach a certain base in Europe in each of the markets in the luxury and top executive category, in order to place the new car in with strong enough dealers. It was necessary to have dealers who were strong enough to be able to do part exchanges, hold minimum stocks, with minimum standards of service, with full training, and purchase the Jaguar Diagnostic System which costs a lot of money at £10,500 a unit.

All this had to be built up so that we could be sure that, when we go into the market with our new car, we have dealers, who can market the cars, and who are of a certain status which gives confidence to the buyer that the cars are being sold, not only as beautiful cars, but also with a back-up service, if required.

We've done a tremendous amount of re-franchising and we've totally changed our importation system in Europe since

John Morgan, the Director of Overseas Sales Operations, and a gifted linguist, joined Jaguar in 1963 and is today one of its elder statesmen. (J.C.)

1984. It was all done in a matter of six months after we broke away from BL. We took Germany away one year before which gave us a very good opportunity to try out on the most difficult market and the first year's results were so encouraging that we had no doubt we were on the right track for the rest of Europe, which fell into place after that.

We've achieved all our objectives in Europe, including Portugal which has just been appointed and already is buzzing away.

We built up the volume in Europe from the very low 2,000s to nearly 5,000 cars and we consider ourselves to be on the right path to handle, I hope, about 10,000 cars. I think we should be as big as the UK. This is very important economically for the company because we do not want to be too dependent on one market. I have always said we should have four solid feet in the world as we used to have before when I was here as Export Director.

I think the new car will appeal tremendously to the Americans. The ones I have shown it to have been very impressed with the beauty of the car; performance is almost secondary as long as it's quiet, smooth and elegant. It has all those features and is much more attractive inside. Our air conditioning system was very Heath Robinson and not popular but the new system is marvellous. Also the diagnostic system where you plug in the JDS and in a second you can find the problem, is superb.

All the drama of owning a car goes out of the window.

The European market is incredibly competitive, more so than anywhere else in the world. To be selling our cars in the jaws of our only competitors is very tough and our car has to be at least as good as theirs. To build the image from something that was a zero and a minus in Germany was obviously very difficult. For example, the name British Leyland is unfortunate because the word elend means misery in German, and that was synonymous with our cars; and everybody used to laugh about it, not only Jaguars but all British cars. I am afraid for the others the image is still there but we have got away from it.

In 1984 Jaguar Deutschland GmbH was set up jointly with Emil Frey the importers for Switzerland and, in fact, the oldest overseas agents. 'I was very pleased I was able to get that through our Board because they have done an absolutely marvellous job'.

With the Series III continuing with the V12 engine for a year or so one cannot help wondering how it will be accepted or whether it will inevitably be thought of as an old model. 'I think it will be thought of as an old model but we have no alternative. The V12 is such an important model to us in Germany where it accounts for 40 per cent of our sales, and is a large percentage in France, Belguim, Holland and Italy. I think we've just to live through that. People who want a V12 are unlikely to be put off by the style of the Series III. Since 1979 it has been such a clean shape'.

To bear out this view of Morgan's, the car that finished second in the styling clinics was not a Mercedes or indeed any of the opposition but the Series III. He even ventured the view that with ABS anti-lock braking, for which there is currently a European vogue, he could sell the car for another five years.

John Morgan does not see cars such as the Granadas, in spite of their increased level of sophistication, as any real competition in these markets. For one thing the Jaguar, even in 2.9 form, will be rather more expensive in Europe. This is described as, 'a marketing decision based on financial considerations'. When a company has a limited production it obviously tries to spread it over the best markets to get the maximum return for its limited

In January 1984, Jaguar shrewdly formed a company jointly with Emil Frey, the long standing Swiss importer, to handle the German market. They built this impressive HQ at Frankfurt. (J.C.)

production if it can sell anywhere. Jaguar intend to aim for full economic profits which means they will be competing with the Mercedes 'S' Series, not the 300s.

The 2.9 will not in fact be available in Germany for the first year and the models available in the various European countries were launched in November to allow, as Derek Waelend explained in the last Chapter, Production to cope gradually. For the same reason the car will not be launched in the States till April. 'The US are not worried at all, they can sell as many Series III's as they can get. Similarly in Europe the car's been going incredibly well. We have no need to discount due to the imminent new model or have any sort of run-out programme. In the UK in the first few days of August 600 cars were registered out of a total stock left in the country of 1,800'.

The intention was to build 800 cars for the UK launch. Morgan wanted 600 for Europe but was not entirely confident he would get them all. Apart from an initial supply, ideally there would then be a continuity of supply in each country in which the car had been launched. The Australians, 'are screaming for cars. The Middle East will have some by Christmas and the Far East will have some by January and February with Japan in May'.

From a background that included Lotus Cars, Roger Putnam joined Jaguar and has enjoyed a meteoric rise to the top of his field. In mid 1986 he graduated from Director of Sales to Director of Sales & Marketing, succeeding Neil Johnson. Putnam's prime responsibility in the recent past has been thoroughly to re-organise the British franchise network. Famous Jaguar garages had been sacked by BL

and Jaguar products mingled in showrooms with all and sundry. This according to the wisdom of BL was the way to sell prestige cars. Jaguar had other thoughts.

We have done a lot in the last four years in separating Jaguar out both in image terms, as far as the prime interface point, which is

Eddie Cheever, Grand Prix driver and member of the TWR Jaguar Group C team, took part in one of the many 'Cricket' videos, not surprisingly combining driving of great verve with his entertaining commentary. (Cricket)

Cricket employed all manner of modern wizardry in producing the videos with cameras mounted in the car and, as we see here, on the outside of the car. (Cricket)

the dealer network, and enhancing the image in bricks and mortar terms. Basically what I set out to do was take away as much as I could any outside influence, over which I had no control, from our franchise network. Jaguar to '82 was fundamentally part of a large multi-franchise situation which had been created in the seventies by the Ryder Report.

Jaguar had lost worldwide a good number of its solus (single make) outlets including the excellent garages like John Coombs at Guildford and Mike Hughes at Beaconsfield – the people who really knew the specialist and luxury car business.

Digressing slightly a moment, I chanced to meet Michael Hughes whilst I was writing this book and he vividly remembered the incident. He had been a Jaguar dealer for 22 years, but was not happy about handling the rest of the British Leyland products following the merging of the companies. Having arranged a meeting with the Leyland people, he merely mentioned this and a young man, who looked no more than about 19, said to

him, 'Right, terminated. Thirty days notice'! That was the end of the conversation!

Within a few hours Hughes had become a Mercedes-Benz dealer and is today one of the largest and most

successful in the country.

Returning to Roger Putnam:

I tried to make the Jaguar franchise as pure as possible. At that time I wasn't to know the horrors that were to afflict the volume

With just over 100 dealers in the U.K. Jaguar are served by a number of highly professional outlets which can concentrate on satisfying present and potential owners. (J.C.)

car side of the business, the massive over-supply situation, and in hindsight I feel a lot better that we moved as quickly and as harshly as we did to separate Jaguar out. There is no way you can successfully market luxury products, specifically cars, if you are in an environment of distressed selling over-supply. Obviously there is a level of luxury and prestige that surrounds a Jaguar which is not enhanced by people giving cars away.

So Jaguar moved from a situation in the UK where they had 300 multi-franchise dealers in 1982 to just over a hundred at the launch of the new car.

The dealers themselves have gone from giving away 17 cars per outlet per year to selling, profitably, an average of almost 70 cars, today.

Our franchise holders have done such a good job of raising their standards and we have finished up with a network that is so strong now that we have managed to operate probably the most successful model run-out that any manufacturer in the UK and possibly anywhere has achieved in the recent past. We are going to have a very smooth run-out and launch situation. We have not had to put a single penny behind the existing product which has been selling very strongly to the end.

We have a basic philosophy, which simply stated, is making money out of satisfying customers.

Solus operations satisfy customers far more than multi-franchise outlets can as we've discovered. A man who buys a Jaguar gets no feeling of inner warmth from the fact that the mechanic is also servicing a Mini. Nor does he feel very much like sitting in a queue in the service reception waiting behind a whole lot of volume car customers. He has invested a lot of money in the product and he expects the same sort of treatment he'd get if he went into a very high class jewellers.

I think the franchise has been held together by the change we tried to bring about in the corporate image. In 1983 our new advertising agency put 'The Legend Grows' theme together for us, which was not terribly intellectually strong but did actually summarise just about everything

we were trying to do. The 'leaper' (leaping Jaguar) was the key to the Legend Grows theme and the 'leaper' then became one of the strongest corporate logos that exists in the car business today.

To find out a little more about the advertising, a field that is Peter

Battam's province at Jaguar, I spoke to John French, Chairman of the F. John French Agency.

My company was retained by Jaguar in early 1983 to rethink the short term future of the company as it stood at that time.

Our role was to maintain the image of the

company which was built very much around the export successes and the improvement in quality. But above all we had to ensure that, what in essence was an old car by that time, could still be perceived to be a quality, luxury car that was still competitive with some of our high-tech foreign import friends.

That we did, initially by creating 'The Legend Grows' slogan. Basically we felt

---

My personal favourite, this advertisement, which the F. John French Agency devised and placed in such media as *The Sunday Times Colour Supplement* and *Country Life*, delightfully pokes fun at the old rivals. (F. John French Agency.)

essor, a tribute to tyre and suspension technology over 5 million miles. From the frozen wastes of , to the merciless Australian outback.

e anti-dive, anti-squat suspension geometry is ed by a self-levelling system, that senses load es. ABS braking with 'anti-yaw' is standard.

ur well-being is also assured. The air conditioning ar-sensing compensation. Seats and door mirrors are power adjusted. The washer jets are electrically heated.

Yet the Sovereign still represents unbeatable value. As do all five new cars, from the 2.9 XJ6 to the opulent Daimler.

Once again, Jaguar have the most sought after currency in the world.

THE NEW JAGUAR SOVEREIGN

that we couldn't get into a product/product argument because there was nothing new about the car. We felt that, with the image of the company built around John Egan and the tremendous PR that was going on plus the increasing market share in America and the definite improvements in quality, we could relaunch the company. It was a year or so before privatisation and we thought that we should capture the history of Jaguar, and the history of Jaguar is C-types, D-types – it was a legend.

We thought that the position of the company, in terms of what it was doing, was becoming legendary and, knowing that the XJ40 was coming, they had a future.

As there were more Daimler saloons in the range than Jaguars, and it's the Jaguar car company, the inbalance was changed and the Sovereign became a Jaguar. We also had the launch of the XJS Cabriolet with the introduction of the 3.6 engine and so there was enough happening in the company which supported an excitement, we felt. We used that and tried to bring the age profile of the traditional Jaguar owner down and to spearhead Sovereign as a conquest car to bring people across from BMW 7 Series.

XJ40 was very much around in those days but was still at the testing stage. We started working on '40' in 1985 and our involvement then was in deciding whether we were purely in the luxury car sector or, with the 2.9 base car, whether we should be in the higher end of the executive car sector as well. Speaking just for the UK, with the volume Jaguar required we had to move out of the pure luxury sector to get those volumes. At the same time, we still wanted to be perceived as a luxury car so it's been a difficult balance. Lots and lots of research has been done at the same time as the car clinic research.

We researched something like twenty different advertising approaches – should the low price be up front, or did we do it more subtly? At the end of the day, we decided the new car was evolutionary rather than revolutionary. We didn't want to lose that 'Jaguarness' but at the same time it had to be perceived to be new and exciting.

URER'S RRP AND CORRECT AT TIME OF GOING TO PRESS, INCLUDE SEAT BELTS, CAR TAX AND VAT. (DELIVERY, ROAD TAX AND NUMBER PLATES EXTRA).

We think there is a strong possibility in large corporate organisations that the Chairman will run a Daimler, the Managing Director a 3.6 Sovereign with the 2.9 Sovereign for the Board. But there is also a large market, which Jaguar traditionally have not had a large share of, and that's the man who, for example, has a small engineering business. He has probably got the only major company car and has been running a Volvo 7 Series, or an Audi 200, or a BMW 5, or a Granada Scorpio, and said to himself, 'can't afford a Jaguar'. Now he can.

Pat Smart, who has the title of Fleet Sales Manager, has been a true Jaguar enthusiast since his days as an apprentice, and at the Birmingham launch was celebrating twenty-five years of manning the company motor show stands. I put it to him that he was now going to have more of a job to do than he had before!

'Exactly! The existing Jaguar customers are delighted with the Sovereign and look as if they are going to purchase the Sovereign 3.6 Automatic in great numbers. Obviously I am hopeful that we can attract another level of management with the XJ6 2.9 and so far every indication is that people are likely to be coming on to us in greater numbers than we have seen since the Mark 2s.'

I asked Pat which manufacturers he saw Jaguar taking business from. 'Hopefully from the people we lost out to in our 'blue' period, i.e. our friends Mercedes and BMW, Audi to a certain extent, and Saab'.

Smart points out that residual values of secondhand Jaguars have improved very considerably recently and the XJ40 promises to have very high residual values. Quite apart from the obvious benefits of this, I think it is significant that leasing costs, which have residual costs as a factor, will be cheaper as a consequence thus reducing the expense of running a Jaguar, thereby increasing new car sales.

With all the euphoria and talk of six month waiting lists like the old days, I asked Robert Collier, UK Sales Director, whether he had a job to do!

Opened just a matter of weeks before the XJ40 launch, Colliers new operation at Sutton Coldfield in the West Midlands is typical of the new breed of dealers, being dedicated solely to Jaguars. (Colliers).

We are looking for quite significant increases in the UK market. I think we have a big job to do. I don't actually believe that any car sells itself. It needs a professional approach to the customer, looking after him or her. That is what they expect. That is what they deserve. That is what they need to get.

There is no question, we've got a cracking car but we don't want to build up an excessive waiting list. We like to satisfy customers within a reasonable time so that they can plan purchase, so that they can feel they are being looked after in the way they should be looked after. As I don't wish to be made redundant, I am totally confident there is more than a good job for all of us!

Enthusiasts are delighted that Jaguar have in recent years, in various forms, returned to the race tracks of the world, including the old hunting ground in France. Roger Putnam: 'I feel that without doubt the motor racing pro-gramme has done a great deal to reduce the average age of our customers'.

I asked Putnam whether he viewed the launch of '40' with any doubts. 'I have no fears. It does everything the current car does just that much better. The breadth of its appeal will give us the strength, to go even further down the age graph. I am very confident we have a better tool to do a better job exploiting what Jaguar do best – that's selling luxury cars.'

I wondered whether Putnam was concerned about the delay in launching and whether the car might now be viewed as a little behind the times.

As we told the dealers back in 1982, some fundamental things had to happen before the car could be launched. One of them was that the customer had to be ready for the car. The second was that the dealer network had to be ready for the car. The third thing was that we had to be ready for the car. As it happens the timing has all been coincidental.

I think we could have had an unmitigated disaster on our hands. Had the car been ready, had we tried to launch it before we had done so much to set the scenery, we could have had an absolute disaster on our hands.

The acceptability of the product, the company, the dealer network, the credibi-lity of us as a management team – all that is absolutely crucial. It's as crucial as the way the car looks and handles.

Putnam refers to having to adopt a holistic approach.

The whole is more than the sum of the parts because it all comes together and has its own in-built synergy.

One of the things that the old network couldn't come to terms with was handling used Jaguars. The minute they got one in it was a financial burden to them and they had to knock it out to a trader, or one of our competitive franchise holders, to a point, that had we launched the car two or three years ago, our network wouldn't have been able to handle the cars coming back in part-exchange. The loyal Jaguar owners, who have been our salvation over the last three years, would have found that they were being offered such ridiculous money in part-exchange for their existing car they couldn't have afforded to change.

Could Jaguar ever grow to the size of Mercedes?

I think I am right in saying that in 1959 Jaguar and Mercedes were pretty similar in size. For a whole variety of reasons, Jaguar stood still or marked time. Bill Lyons' son had been killed and he had no successor, in the sixties the amalgamations happened and so on. During the period that Jaguar marked time and possibly went backwards,

Mercedes were achieving a nice 15 per cent growth per annum, which has taken them through to the sort of volumes that they are making today.

'In the last four years we have trebled what Jaguar were doing in the late seventies. That sort of growth obviously must cease but if we can actually achieve a nice steady 15 per cent growth ourselves simply by exploiting business that Jaguar understands, then with the saloon, the grand tourer and, eventually, a sports car we can quite satisfactorily grow this company in line with our requirements and our shareholders' requirements, and remain uniquely Jaguar into the 1990s.

I expressed my surprise that Roger Putnam, so obviously an executive in the modern mould, should see a significance in the Jaguar's past.

When I said that 'The Legend Grows' theme was a key platform for all sorts of things, it is because 'legend' has no time. It is historic, present and future. I think that's what Jaguar is all about.

In spite of all that we are doing today with CAD-CAM and robotics and that sort of thing, philosophically Jaguar hasn't changed at all. We still follow the three pillars of marketing wisdom that Bill Lyons established from the outset.

He set out to build a car that had elegant, unique styling. It had to have engineering excellence and last, but not least, it offered superb value for money. Nothing we are doing has in anyway altered those three pillars of wisdom.

The other thing you must add to that today is that you must build a car that starts, runs and stops at the owner's behest, and not the car's!

Chapter 8
Roaring to go

We have looked at the design and development of the car, now we take a look in some detail at the eventual specification and performance of the XJ6, Sovereign and Daimler plus some initial driving impressions and Press reaction.

Great play has been made of the fact that only the names and the badge on the steering wheel have been carried over from the Series III, which continues with the V12 engine for another year or so.

The basic model, if you can ever call a Jaguar basic, is entitled the XJ6. It is offered with either the 2.9-litre or 3.6-litre AJ6 engines with Getrag five-speed manual transmission as standard. As an extra cost option, ZF four-speed automatic transmission can be specified. Standard mechanical features include power assisted steering, adjustable steering column, a stainless steel exhaust, impact-absorbing wrap-around bumpers, power boost assisted four-wheel disc brakes, a comprehensive tool kit and rear door child locks.

Optional items on the XJ6 include cruise control, anti-lock braking, a limited-slip differential and ride levelling.

Externally the XJ6 is distinguishable immediately from the front by the twin traditional round headlamps. At the rear differences are rather more subtle. The badging on the 2.9 is in open script whereas the 3.6-litre models have the names engraved in black on a silver rectangular background. These are the only external distinguishing features.

Optional external items include alloy wheels and a metallic paint finish. Internally the XJ6 is fitted with herringbone tweed cloth seat trim with leather as an option. Standard specification consists of figured walnut veneer, tinted glass, central locking, including boot and petrol filler, electric windows and electrically adjustable mirrors.

A novel feature is the fact that when the car is locked, all the windows and the electric sunshine roof, if fitted, are also automatically closed.

Further standard items include an electrically heated rear window, with timer, front and rear courtesy light delay, an illuminated door/ignition key, electrically heated windscreen washers, kerb illumination lights on all doors and an electronic stereo radio/cassette player with four speakers, plus a number of other features one takes for granted these days.

Optional interior and electrical items consist of air conditioning, headlamp power washers, eight-way electrically adjustable front seats, heated front seats, electric sunroof, rear window sunblinds, heated door lock barrels and a radio with no less than six speakers!

The more up-market model, destined to be the most popular, if Series III experience is anything to go by, is the Jaguar Sovereign.

It obviously shares all the XJ6 features and a number which are optional on that model. It is available with the two sizes of engine but the ZF automatic transmission is standard with the Getrag manual box a no-cost option, to use the current jargon.

Cruise control, anti-lock braking and ride levelling are all standard with the limited-slip differential optional. Met-

On XJ6 models the distinctive grille is mounted between twin halogen headlamps, and the black deep section wraparound bumpers are surrounded by a chromium plated steel capping. (P.H.P.)

Jaguar Sovereign and Daimler models are distinguished by the single headlamps and are equipped with heated jets for the headlamp power wash. (P.H.P.)

allic paint, what are termed 'styled headlamps', double coachline and stainless steel door glass frames are standard with alloy wheels an option. Standard interior and electrical features include air conditioning, heated door mirrors, the headlamp washers, electrically adjustable seats, rear head restraints and the six speaker radio. Optional items are as for the XJ6, if not already standard, with the addition of cloth trim at no extra cost.

The Daimler, which apparently has no model name, is immediately identifiable by the famous fluted top to the radiator grille and bootlid plinth.

It is offered with just the larger engine and with the ZF transmission though, again the Getrag manual 'box is available. Mechanically it is as its lesser brethren but with the limited-slip differential. Externally it enjoys the alloy wheels, a single coachline with a chrome body side-moulding and most interestingly, the neutral density rear and side light lenses.

Other standard features are reading lamps in the rear pillars, heated front seats, electric sunshine roof and those splendid fold down walnut veneer picnic tables that seem so much a part

The opulent Daimler version is instantly recognised by its famous fluted grille at the front and similarly fluted boot plinth at the rear. (P.H.P.)

The body-colour front spoiler with its black lower section blends tastefully into the overall styling. (P.H.P.)

Left: This photograph, with the Daimler XJ40 on the left and Series III on the right, illustrates the considerably revised front end treatment between the old and the new. (P.H.P.)

of a traditional Jaguar saloon. Interior specification is completed by what is described as 'unique Daimler-style seats incorporating a centre cubby box and additional storage in a pull down arm rest'. Options are listed at just the heated door lock barrels and rear window sunblinds.

All these specifications are for the UK models and may vary in detail from country to country to suit local tastes or domestic legislation. As to costs, again UK, the new cars reflect extraordinary value for money in true Lyons style. The manual XJ6 2.9 costs £16,495 and the

manual XJ6 3.6 £18,495. The 2.9 and 3.6 Sovereigns are £22,295 and £24,995 respectively, whilst the Daimler is £28,495. The major XJ6 cost options are air conditioning at £1,250 and anti-lock braking at £1,050.

As anyone who restores an older Jaguar knows, body corrosion has always been one of the company's weaker points. In the new car all seams are sealed with a robot-applied compound and extensive use is made of zinc-coated steels in critical underbody areas and cavities. The body-in-white is primed electrophoretically by totally immersing a negatively charged shell into a tank of positively charged primer. The underside is coated with a tough sealant with an extra coat of anti-chip on the sills. All box members are wax-injected, using hot wax applied by a spinning lance for good penetration.

The rear ride levelling referred to earlier is powered by an engine-driven pump, actually shared with the braking system although the latter takes priority! Struts are used rather than conventional dampers to provide the height correction and each strut contains a gas accumulator which is hydraulically pressurised. Suspension height variations are gauged by an electro-mechanical sensor linked to the rear right-hand wishbone.

'Twenty-five seconds after a load change the system's electronic control unit (ECU) 'decides' the change is a long term one and not a transient difference due to cornering roll and it allows pressure to be fed to the strut to correct the height. The change is made in up to a maximum of 20 seconds – usefully faster than a self-powered system,' states a Jaguar handout.

If the engine stops, the engine-driven hydraulic pump will obviously do likewise but if braking is still needed the pressure accumulator has sufficient stored hydraulic energy to provide between eight and twenty stops dependent on pedal pressures applied. This compares with two to four stops with a vacuum servo.

Right: Rear views show the different tail treatment, and on the XJ40, in the foreground, the rear quarterlight is separate from the rear door, unlike the Series III (P.H.P.)

Below: The XJ6 has a single coachline and, together with the Sovereign, flush wheel trims both for reasons of style and aerodynamics. (J.C.)

132

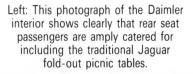

The brakes have 11.6 in (295 mm) diameter ventilated discs at the front and 10.9 in (278 mm) solid discs at the rear each with an integral handbrake drum. Calipers are fist-type with circuits split front/rear.

Inside one finds the usual stalk controls. The left-hand one operates the indicators, headlamp dip/flash and horn. The right-hand one operates the two-speed wipers, flick and intermittent wipe, screen washers and, when fitted, the headlamp washers. The switches for the lights, fog lamps and hazard warning lights are positioned to the left of the column whilst the trip computer and optional cruise control are to be found on the right.

On the centre console are located switches for the interior lamp, map light, rear window heater and central locking. Mirror and window controls reside on the doors and the seat control, when specified, is adjacent to one's knees on the side of the centre console.

Thankfully, Jaguar plumped for a traditional circular analogue speedometer and tacho rather than following the current vogue for gimmickry. Both are electronic, eliminating the need for cables, which are just another item to go wrong. The tamperproof electronic odometer has a two-year memory should the battery be disconnected.

Apart from the usual warning lights, the instrument panel also displays the setting of the automatic gear selector and, if required, an additional digital speed reading.

The oil pressure, battery voltage, temperature and fuel gauges display as vacuum fluorescent bar graphs with different levels for concern being illustrated by a change in colour. The

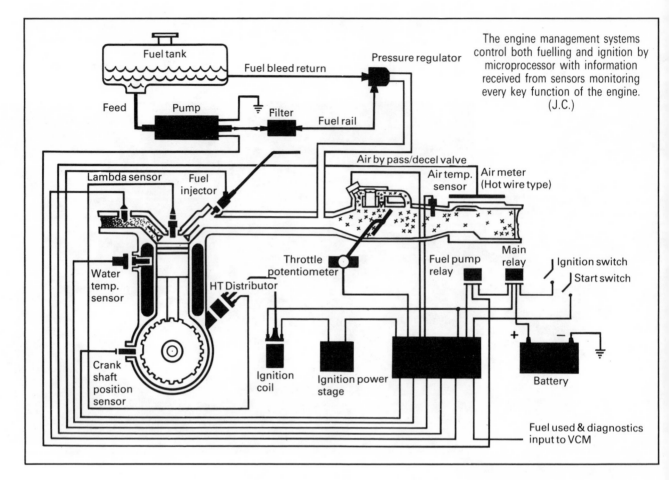

The engine management systems control both fuelling and ignition by microprocessor with information received from sensors monitoring every key function of the engine. (J.C.)

small dot matrix television screen situated to the right of the column is known as the Vehicle Condition Monitor (VCM).

The trip computer operates on command under three headings. Under 'time' one is informed of average speed, time taken and time to go. Under 'distance' it tells you mileage so far, mileage to go and range based on average fuel consumption and fuel level. Finally under 'fuel' it acquaints you with average consumption, consumption at that very moment and fuel consumed. Readings can be shown in Imperial or metric.

An ambient air temperature sensor, located in the front spoiler, activates the heated windscreen washer nozzles, and headlamp ones if fitted, should the temperature drop below 5°C (41°F). Headlamps are automatically switched

off with the engine as you expect today, but additionally a warning light reminds one that the sidelights are still on. The mirrors are electrically heated on the Sovereign and Daimler models and are timed, like the rear window, to operate for 20 minutes only. A 'panic' button in the centre console locks and shuts everything.

In the event of an impact, the doors are automatically unlocked and fuel supply is terminated. The driver can isolate the rear locks to prevent the little horrors escaping!

The four interior lamps remain on for 15 seconds upon opening a door unless cancelled by switching on the ignition. If a door is left open, battery drain is minimised by an automatic cut-out after two minutes.

Running costs have been a major consideration and service intervals are

now set at 7,500 and 15,000 miles, and it is claimed that the amount of work required at these regular services has been significantly reduced. 'Over 50,000 miles,' Jaguar state, 'the new saloons incur only 13.95 hours of labour charges. On similar luxury saloons, the equivalent figure can be as high as 20.00 for routine maintenance.

Components have been designed with speedier repair or replacement in mind. Whereas it took 3.30 hours to replace a Series III fuel tank, it now takes 1.80 hours. The replacement of all four brake discs used to take 9.00 hours with the inboard rears on the old car. It now takes a little over two hours. The company has worked closely with the insurance industry's research centre at Thatcham to optimise repair techniques.

Further reducing the costs of running

a Jaguar has been the policy, since taking back the parts operations from BL, of pricing as competitively as possible. Indeed since the boxes have again carried the Jaguar name, items have actually come down in price.

I asked Mike Walker, Regional Parts Executive, about availability. He expressed his answer in this way. 'I dare to talk to Service Managers and ask them if we are looking after them! Two years ago I would have been very scared! In fact 94 per cent of all parts we will deliver first time and we have a Customer Service Section which will find the part if it is anywhere in the world'.

After hearing so much about the XJ40 and talking to so many people about it, I was naturally very keen to drive examples to see whether all the claims and optimism was really justified or merely hype.

them to invite me and approached the task with some excitement.

To begin I selected a 3.6 because performance interests me rather more than economy, especially as Shell were kindly providing the petrol! I thought I would start with an automatic to find out whether the 'J gate' was a gimmick or not.

My first reaction was desperate disappointment and great concern. The car rolled around and there was considerable noise from the rear of the car. The performance seemed adequate rather than impressive. My concern was simply for the future of Jaguar. The distinguished Scottish journalist shar-

The author takes a break at Kildrummy during his high speed dash around the quiet, beautiful and challenging roads to the Scottish Highlands. (P. Skilleter)

spectacular scenery of the Highlands to the coffee stop. Here, thankfully, we managed to change cars.

The new car was a revelation. The ride and level of grip were superb. The whole car now inspired tremendous confidence and what was particularly impressive was the way it changed direction so much better than the Series III which did tend to feel its weight when sweeping through a series of bends. The new car could be flicked around without excessive roll. It gave the impression of being much lighter.

This 3.6-litre, being a manual version, felt much more lively. Using the 'box to the full through the mountains, the car became an absolute joy and felt like a true sporting Jaguar for the eighties and beyond. I recalled that Jim Randle had assured me that he had not lost sight of the fact that a Jaguar should be a performance car as well as a refined car. I revelled in pushing the car harder and harder.

One must give full credit for an ideal choice of location. The roads were quiet and we experienced most conditions including twisty country roads, steep mountain passes, rough sections and fast straight dual carriageways. In all conditions the car was superbly impressive and one mentally congratulated the hundreds, or perhaps, more accurately, thousands of people involved.

I dare not state in print how fast we went but would illustrate the speed, smoothness and silence by this anecdote. Talking a week or two later to a photographer I often work with, we were discussing the car. He had been to Scotland a week before me. Up there he was being driven by a journalist colleague and was busy, head down, changing films and sorting his equipment. When they arrived back at base, the driver asked him if he was aware what speed they had been doing. He thought probably 80/90 mph. they had been cruising at 130 plus!

After a 200 mile morning trip and lunch, we took out a 2.9 manual and inevitably found it slower, but the car

As will be mentioned in Chapter 9, the PR department set-up what were termed 'Ride and Drive' sessions in Scotland for the Press to try the car in September. I managed to persuade

ing the car with me, and I, stopped. Quickly we discovered that the nearside rear shock absorber was completely 'shot'. We soldiered on a hundred miles through the fabulously

Left: The side view is particularly stylish. It is significant that one needs to look twice, if not thrice, to distinguish the new car from its predecessor. (P.H.P.)

The XJ40 rear three-quarter view, with perhaps slight discernable Rolls-Royce influence, works well with a deeper boot for improved capacity and a small, discreet spoiler lip to the boot lid. (P.H.P.)

The new Dunlop TD tyres are wider and squatter than those of the Series III, their low aspect ratio giving very good cornering ability together with a 130 mph speed rating. (P.H.P.)

was far from a slouch. Using the gears produced a very lively performance and it was very happy to cruise at high speeds with refinement. Naturally it shared its larger brother's attributes in the handling and roadholding departments. On both cars, the brakes were simply the best I have ever experienced.

The interiors are pure Jaguar tradition with relatively unobtrusive modern gadgetry. The computer is an amusing toy, though one French TV man I spoke to complained vociferously that the small screen was entirely out of keeping in a Jaguar!

I concluded the day with a brief run in the automatic Daimler on my own so that there was no-one to worry about terrifying! I pushed the car very hard, far harder than one would normally drive even when in a frantic hurry. I would like to try one on the track but certainly on the road the car exhibited no vices. It was, in fact, very safe and very exciting – a real driver's car.

As to criticisms; I am hard pressed to think of any. One car we drove suffered from wind noise in the driver's door area. The power steering is an improvement but for me, personally, is still too assisted. Finally, one feature I positively hated was the new method of operating the indicators which required a second action to cancel them. I gather a number of other 'muttering rotters' felt likewise and there was some talk of changing to a more conventional set-up. I hope Jaguar do!

With regard to the 'J gate', I was very ready to sneer and dismiss it as a gimmick. I liked it. The 'manual' change allows one to play tunes with ease on an automatic and is very fast and easy to use.

As to fuel consumption, my results may make amusing reading but are hardly fair comment. The 3.6 manual with pretty brisk driving over a long distance recorded, so the computer told me, 22 mpg which is far from disappointing remembering the terrain and manner of driving. The 2.9, ironically, returned only 18 mpg but it

should be stated I was using high revs a good deal and the figure was improving all the time, as I drove more normally.

The Daimler figure should certainly not be taken seriously – 10.9 mpg!

Finally I spoke to other journalists of various nationalities to ascertain their reaction and see if I was biased in my favourable reaction. Being a Jaguar enthusiast and patriot, had I perhaps willed it to be good and were my conclusions rational?

To a man, they had nothing but praise for the car.

* * * * *

Let us now take a brief look at what the Press wrote about the car upon its announcement.

By craftily borrowing an XJ6 from a dealer, rather than waiting for a factory Press car, *Autocar* published on 15 October what they claimed to be a 'world exclusive' – the first road test.

Likening the long wait for a product, that was known to be imminent for some time, to a child waiting for Christmas, *Autocar* stated that, 'just like the best Christmas, it is well worth the wait'.

Having mentioned that the 'aluminium-alloy-cased in-line six' is the 'only such combination in production worldwide', the magazine stated that BMW's M635i claimed '81.8 bhp per litre, to the Jaguar's 61.6 Partly because it is known that there is plenty more development to come from this engine, this emphasises that the aim of the XJ6 in its present guise remains the production of smooth, refined power'.

Not surprisingly they were impressed by the traditional Jaguar value for money and new electrical system. 'This Low Current Earth Line Switching system is in fact one large step nearer

the Multiplex electrics of the near future. Add to all that a price of £18,495 for the 3.6 manual gearbox XJ6 tested, and you seem to have a Coventry cat among the national and international pigeons.

'In bald figures,' wrote the testers, 'XJ6 3.6 as tested (without too many of the weight-adding extras) weighs 4 per cent less than the XJ6 Series 3 4.2 manual . . . has nearly 8 per cent more DIN horsepower, and according to Jaguar's wind tunnel quotations has 10 per cent less drag. So it ought to be both quicker and more efficient, in spite of the 15 per cent smaller capacity'.

They found that it *was* quicker, recording a 0-60 mph time of 7.4 seconds, achieving the standing quarter mile in 15.8 seconds and posting a mean maximum speed of 137 mph. Driving hard they covered 18.6 mpg,

more gentle motoring yielding 26.9 mpg with the average working out at 22.8 mpg. 'Judged more subjectively,' they opined, 'the manual 3.6 is a much more entertaining car to drive quickly than its forerunner. It feels eager, in a way that was not quite so obvious in the 4.2' Emphasising the point, they felt

that the new car was, 'enticingly sporting in its power delivery.'

Autocar disliked the horn note and thought the seats needed to give more lateral location. However they approved of the air conditioning system and especially the three-stage humidity control. 'This feature really does help to

eliminate the 'dry-eye' phenomenon often associated with other automotive air conditioning systems and should be particularly welcomed by wearers of contact lenses'.

They concluded that, it becomes clear that Jaguar's biggest problem with the new car will be meeting the demand'.

The 2.9-engined cars are distinguished by open script badging and the 3.6-litre cars have plaque-style badges, whilst the Sovereign is further recognisable by the charcoal applique rear number plate panel. (J.C.)

Gordon Cruickshank writing in *Motor Sport* was similarly generous in his praise for most aspects of the car. 'But to this writer ar least,' he stated in the November 1986 issue, 'it seems as if an opportunity has been missed. It is true that the XJ40 is very obviously a Jaguar, but it is so close to the Series III in proportion as to seem only a year or two in advance of it. That is not to say that it is not attractive – it is both nicely proportioned and well detailed, a very handsome car indeed, but any design has a limited shelf-life, and this one looks now as it it had appeared two years ago. In four years time it will have fallen noticeably behind its BMW and Mercedes rivals. Let us hope that the conservatism of its customers will continue to offset this.'

He concluded by saying that the XJ6 was, 'luxury performance in its most relaxed form – despite my carp about the styling, Jaguar's new offering deserves its place as the Series III successor'.

Much as I respect Gordon's opinions, he is, and readily admits, to being very much in the minority with his views on the styling and I would remind him that the original XJ6 managed, by force of circumstance, to last 18 years and it was the Series III that was finishing second to the new car in all those styling clinics, ahead of the German boxes. The new car, with updating revisions, a number of which are already finalised, is scheduled to last just half that period, that is, nine years.

A brief look at other publications yields the following reaction. *Motor*, under the heading 'A Star is Re-born', introduced the car stating, 'with its smooth six-cylinder engine and a brilliant ride/handling compromise, it's arguably the most comfortable car in the world.'

Steve Cropley, the Editor of *Car*,

Ride levelling units, fitted to the Sovereign and Daimler models, cope with maximum payload or towing weight, and heated door mirrors help to maintain clear rearward visibility in inclement conditions. (P.H.P.)

best, roadholding and handling the match of the rest and better than most'.

He felt the steering was too light, the trip computer beyond him and polished wood inappropriate in a modern car, but 'both engines impressed mightily. There is only one word to sum up the new XJ40 (I suspect it's going to be called that by the public, no matter how hard Jaguar try and push the old names): brilliant'.

As to newspaper headlines: John Langley's article in *The Daily Telegraph* was headed 'The new Jaguar with the old look'; Robert Glenton's in *The Sunday Express*, 'This Sovereign will still be king in the year 2000'; *The Times* – 'Sleek and stylish Jaguar models retain old names'; Colin Dryden expressed his opinion in *The Sunday Telegraph* that this was 'A Jag worth waiting for'.

Further headlines were: *The Star* – 'UNCAGED – A new Jag purrs out'; *The Independent* – 'Jaguar launches into new market'; *The Financial Times* – 'A fast but narrow lane'; *Today* – 'Jaguar roar in with a show stopper'; *Daily Mail* – 'The car the world's been waiting for'; and *Daily Express* – 'King of the big cats'.

A few days after the launch, *The Daily Telegraph* printed the following:

JAGUAR BLACK MARKET – Jaguar is trying to kill off a developing black market for its new range. Frustrated buyers have been offering up to £3,000 over the £16,500 minimum list price for the new XJ6, Sovereign and Daimler models, for which there is a six-months waiting list. Jaguar has said it will cut off supplies to dealers who profiteer.

Presumably there is no sincerer form of flattery than a black market. That, I suppose, in the real world is the ultimate compliment.

writing in his page entitled 'Agenda', reckoned, 'the car isn't perfect, but it is conclusively the best of the only three cars you can seriously list as contenders for the title of the world's best saloon car'.

Mike McCarthy, writing in *Autosport*, agreed. 'Dynamically the XJ40 is the best saloon in the world, and sorry Messrs. Rolls Royce, Mercedes-Benz, BMW, Cadillac et al. Comfort levels are supreme, refinement better than the

Above left: Manoeuvring an XJ40 into
the headquarters of the Institute of
Mechanical Engineers, for Jim
Randle's presentation of his paper was
no easy matter and entailed the
construction of a special rig to rotate
the car on to its side. (J.C.)

Above right: Once on its side, the car
had to be pushed, with only a hair's
breadth to spare, down the corridor
and through a series of doors. (J.C.)

Inside the conference room, the XJ40
provided the backdrop for a number
of speakers who gave papers,
commencing with Jim Randle (J.C.)

Roger Putnam, Sales and Marketing Director, becomes a star of stage and screen as he introduces one of the many trade launches. (Cricket)

Following the launch speeches and the video, the main 'reveal' begins with the central screen being tilted towards the audience. (Cricket)

The climax of the dramatic 'reveal' drew spontaneous and lengthy applause on every occasion. (Cricket)

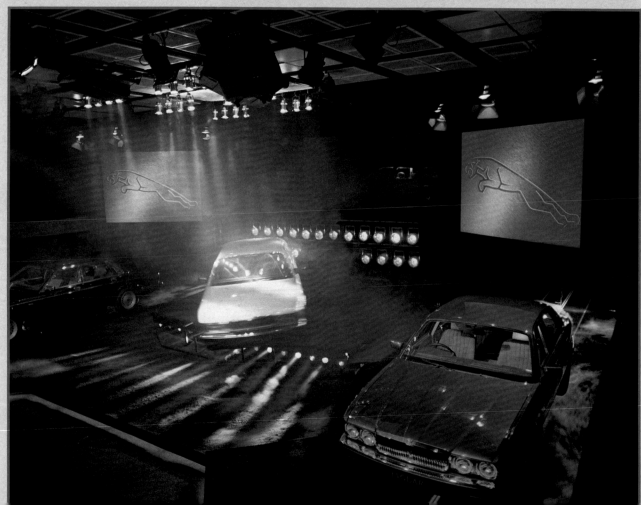

On the sign on the car:

16th SEPTEMBER 1983
THE 1st (FOUR) XJ40s
Who said it couldn't be done?

Sir John celebrates with colleagues the completion of the fourth XJ40, so the sign says, but in fact five SEPs and around 14 FEPs had been completed by this date. (J.C.)

With a fine team of Directors assisting him, Sir John Egan is today firmly in the driving seat of Jaguar Cars plc, from August 1984 a separate, privatised company and Britain's biggest manufacturing dollar earner. (J.C.)

At the new model's Motor Show début a goodly number of XJ40s shared the simple but stylish stand with examples of XJS and a V12 Series III, seen here in the background. (J.C.)

The V12 engined XJR-6, which so nearly took Derek Warwick to the world sports car title in 1986, here puts in an appearance on Jaguar's Motor Show stand. (J.C.)

Chapter 9
Launching the Legend

Having designed and developed a car, having organised one's manufacturing facilities and formed a marketing plan, it is necessary to launch the product with maximum impact. On the one hand it was of obvious importance for Jaguar to launch successfully with XJ40 being vital to the company's very existence. On the other hand, the excitement naturally engendered by the launch of a new Jaguar meant that to some extent the publicity would be self-generating and there would not be a need to advertise heavily initially.

Before launching a car, a name has to be chosen for it and a great deal of thought goes into that seemingly simple task. In the middle of 1986, I discussed this with David Boole, Director of Communications and Public Affairs, and asked if it was going to be known as an XJ40 or a Series IV?

If you go back to 1980, the last thing we dreamed of doing was carrying over the name. But because of the rehabilitation of XJ6 and the tremendous following it has got in the States and other markets, due to

the improvements in quality and reliability, it seemed pretty nonsensical for us to do anything other than call the new car XJ6. It will not be Series IV because that would have implied just an update to an existing product.

The launch is really quite unique as far as those of us who have worked in the British car industry are concerned, because on every other occasion that we can think of in the past, when we've been involved in a new car launch, we've been really quite desperate to distance the new car from its predecessor. Usually what has happened is that the car that has been sold by the company for a number of years has either stopped selling or is slowing down very badly or, in some extreme occasions, has been withdrawn from the market several months previously. We're launching this car on the back of ever increasing demand for the car it will replace.

Launching a car is virtually a science in its own right today and very much more than merely giving a lunch to the Press and showing the car to the public at a motor show. Some manufacturers

spend many millions on the launch and fly the Press to exotic locations where they are wined and dined lavishly and have gifts showered upon them.

The build-up to the XJ40 launch was rather like a military campaign and required precision planning. Not surprisingly a vast number of people were involved in many different ways. The task of co-ordinating all these elements and the operation fell to Chris Baker who had been the UK Sales Manager formerly.

In February, 1986 he was appointed Project Manager for the launch and here he explains his role and describes the many events organised by his colleagues.

I have acted as a combination of Project Leader and of safety net, and had to handle the myriad 'Oh, and another thing' queries and questions that crop up, as you are thinking of avoiding the problems as well as reaping the opportunites. So we have had a a very intensive six or nine month period during which we have been trying very hard to ensure that we left as little to

chance as possible, all very much within a ruthlessly constrained budget.

Various people had already evolved plans for their area of responsibility.

Firstly it was a matter of picking up an embryonic timing plan which summarised all the Sales & Marketing and Public Relations activities on particular key dates. There was a certain amount of original thinking and planning going on but also there were clearly a number of things we'd had to do a long time previously.

For example, the launch film was two or three years old by that stage. We'd been shooting footage since about '83. A number of things were already a long way down the track. The Motor Show is another example. There is an awful lot you have to commit months in advance, in terms of space and position and that sort of thing. Even back in March we were struggling to get what we regarded as the right location for our stand.

One of the things we've tried extraordinarily hard to do is not to bog the whole thing down in a hopeless bureaucracy. We've tried to work on the principle of making sure a person knows what his job is and then making sure on a monthly or weekly basis that he has done it. We've published minutes of meetings and briefing notes together with a timing plan.

This timing plan lists a series of key actions which are a distillation of what are, in some people's cases, several pages of timings of their own. For example, the print and advertising people will have all sorts of dates for when the brochure goes on press and when it's bound and cut, and all the rest.

In March there were previews held for the UK Dealer Council, European importer principals, overseas distributor principals and the USA Dealer Council. With regard to the last-named, Baker comments that 'at that stage they were still more than a year away from launch and a number of them were laying down mega-bucks putting brand new luxury facilities up. Clearly they believed the new car was going to do the

business but they would sleep a hell of a lot better at nights if they'd seen and driven the cars'.

During April the employees at each of the plants were given, in turn, a preview and in mid-June all employees were shown a video on the car. In the same month the Purchasing Director, Pat Audrain, presented the XJ40 to the suppliers.

In the middle of August a similar presentation was put on, not only for Jaguar's own union officials, but also all the full-time local, regional and national officials of the unions recognised by Jaguar.

Chris Baker describes that as, 'A very sincere and well meant attempt to communicate well in advance how crucial the project was, how it fitted in in marketing terms and also to acknowledge to them that they had a considerable rôle to play. It was vital that they were aware, at all levels, just how critical it was to the company, the fact that we were changing 80 per cent of the model range in a single fell swoop.'

Baker describes himself as a marketing man with little or no experience of industrial relations, 'but I was very struck, firstly by how positive and enthusiastic they were and also by the way they responded to how we saw the car. They were very keen for Press Packs and wanted us to arrange test drives for their General Council members and head office staff. This was not so much because they were prospective customers, though undoubtedly one or two of the senior union members would be, but because they were so enthusiastic about the car, they wanted to spread the word'.

On 26 August Jim Randle and colleagues gave a technical paper on the design and development to the Institution of Mechanical Engineers. Jonathan Heynes recalls that when his father gave a similar paper on the XJ6 he wished to have a car on show and this necessitated taking a window out of the building, stopping the traffic and lowering a car in by crane!

Not surprisingly, Jim Randle was equally keen to have his car on show. By taking a paper cut-out of the side plan of the car full size through the main doors of the Institute's headquarters in Birdcage Walk, London, it was found that the car could just navigate the corridors and bends, et cetera, with a hair's breadth to spare!

Stuart Spencer, whose responsibility it was to get the car in, explained what it involved:

I took the problem to George Mason, a brilliant guy, Superintendent of the Experimental shop and told him we had to turn the car on its side, couldn't go outside the dimensions of the car, had to take the stresses, etc., and be able to move it on its side. He, together with Dave White, Bill Reid and Gerry Costello, built a rig which rotated the car and then became a chassis with castors.

We built a complete plywood mock-up of the Institute, at Whitley, and walked a car through a few times to prove it could be done. A truck then had to be found that would take the length of the car but was also the correct height to be level with the top of the steps of the Institute. The pavement sloped as well which didn't help!

The floors of the building were sheeted with plywood and steel and after one heart stopping moment the car was manoeuvred in with nothing to spare, and the event was a great success. The police were tremendously helpful and I couldn't resist persuading one of them to give Jim Randle the first ever parking ticket for an XJ40!

The UK Trade launch began the same day and continued till 2 September. Chris Baker describes the format.

We had a neatly combined pattern of live speakers, primarily Roger Putnam, interspersed with video modules, but concluding with the Chairman.

Right at the beginning we said wouldn't it be nice to have more involvement of the plant. It's very easy to put a big glossy show on up at the front in our special events theatre and conference area ignoring the fact that there was the good old

A friendly policeman is persuaded by Stuart Spencer to give Randle the XJ40's first parking ticket and Jim must be one of the few people to ever find the experience an amusing one! (J.C.)

fashioned business of making motor cars going on at the back. So we had Derek Waelend doing a sort of link in from the 'studio' – with aerial shots of the plants – and then we cut to each of the plant directors, who were interviewed by Derek.

That gave us a perfect opportunity to take the audience through the level of nitty-gritty that frankly you wouldn't be able to do normally because it would be too tedious without lots of visuals.

So we set the scene at the beginning of the presentation. We gave ourselves a little

excuse to give a brief pre-reveal of the car, following which it proceeded on logically that having glimpsed the hero of the story, which is how we described it, let's talk a bit about the 'background to the future'. So we talked about the development and then Derek introduced each of the Plant Directors.

Gerry Lawlor at Castle Bromwich talked about the reduction in body panels, the new paint process, and the kind of quality levels being achieved. Eynon Thomas, at Radford, was able to talk about Statistical Process Control, the asset of a trained and skilled workforce and the family spirit. Finally at Browns Lane, Wal Turner, standing in the pilot build facility, talked about the assembly process and quality audits.

Following the videos, the screen itself pivoted forward to a horizontal position, with a car mounted on it, to the accompaniment of generous amounts of dry ice and suitably stirring music rising to a climax.

An outside firm that played a very large part in all the launch events – indeed, has played an important role assisting Jaguar with communications both internally and externally in the last few years – was Cricket Communications. As John Davies, a director, explained to me, they produced the excellent, and appropriately tailored, videos that accompanied all the events, originated ideas, wrote scripts and with their dramatic 'reveal' stage-managed most of the events.

With the assistance of the 'Cricket' videos, Roger Putnam tells his trade launch audience a story, the story of Jaguar's future. (Cricket)

Putnam cross-examines Derek Waelend on the pertinent subjects of quality and reliability, and between them they make a convincing double-act!. (Cricket)

The UK Trade were followed by two days of the same ritual with the fleet and leasing purchasers together with one or two key government purchasers.

With these presentations completed it was the turn of John Morgan's European dealers; 650 of them in six days. We spoke about it just a few days before it was due to happen.

We are taking them first to Hagley Hall for a gala dinner in the evening with their wives and then we bring them back to Browns Lane for the splendid presentation next morning. The reason we are doing it here – it's funny it goes back to Sir William's day when he always did it here apart from the XJ6 which we had to do in London – is that we decided we would spend all the money on this building rather than do it in hotels. So we can now use our own factory time-after-time for various meetings and it has certainly already paid off. We have got the most sophisticated electronics in this place that you could have anywhere in Britain, with laser beams and video and so on.

We will put up a large marquee for dining and a display of cars plus visuals of all the features like JDS and the dashboard. We are keeping the prices quiet and won't announce those in each country until the day before the launch. The actual launch is being done in the English language, taking

out sections which are not applicable to them – like the 2.9 will not be discussed with the Germans because we're not selling it there for the first year. We shall have instantaneous translation in the languages of each country.

They will go back totally clued up and then we begin training courses on the continent, salesman's training courses, service training courses. We've already trained the trainers.

Because there is an international show on in Paris, we shall do a 'reveal' there during the last days. I am bringing 40 of the top German dealers to England with their wives and they will be staying at Brocket Hall for a few days before the launch. We will then take them to the various launches at the London dealers and I am giving a party at the Royal Thames afterwards.

Following John Morgan's European contingent, the show rolled on for dealers from New Zealand, Japan, Australia, the Middle East, Far East and Canada. Chris Baker takes up the story again. 'Then we had the Americans, 160 of them plus wives and Leonia [US Jaguar HQ] people. They were with us three days and had a combination of trade launch, factory visits and leisure time. They had already been together in Switzerland for three days before that, so they had a real group ambience by the time they reached us!'

After these trade launches it was the employees' turn when Jaguar staged

Robert Collier, the U.K. Sales Director, drives the point home to the dealers who must be convinced before they can be expected to deliver the sales. (Cricket)

Amongst much dry ice and stirring music, cars emerge either side of the screen as it tilts towards a horizontal position, 'revealing' a further XJ40. (Cricket)

The Chairman, now an immensely experienced performer, closes the dynamic launch presentation. (Cricket)

four 'J Days', as they were entitled, at the National Exhibition Centre. All Jaguar employees and their families plus employees of the dealerships were invited to attend these remarkable events which were organised by Mike Kinski who has the title of Manager, Human Resources. 'We believe that the people who build, sell and service the cars are equally as important as our dealers and our customers, and we wanted to launch our cars as professionally to our employees as we have done to our dealers and the Press.

'It's good communication, but it is more than that. It's all about involving the families in 'the pride of achievement' which is what the 'J Days' are all about.

'We've had 28,000 people attend over four days. We are ecstatic with the results and the employees have gone away very happy with what they've seen.'

I attended the final day of this remarkable event, which had been planned, designed, co-ordinated and project managed by Cricket, and there was no doubt that this was very intelligent management. Representatives from each of the Jaguar departments were there explaining such developments as IVER, the In Vehicle Event Recorder – a boot-mounted

device fitted to certain selected cars to gather information on usage – and laser technology – used for example for marking, measuring and cutting – with tremendous enthusiasm, commitment and, above all, pride to their fellow colleagues. The spectacular started with a dynamic video, the dramatic 'reveal' which extracted instant and spontaneous applause, and concluded with a short speech by a member of senior management, in my case Robert Collier.

Those attending then wandered around the hall examining the exhibits and talking to those manning the stands – employees like Mike Deadman, who was explaining, and demonstrating, the part lasers will be playing in Jaguar's future. Apart from the in-house stands, firms like Dunlop had taken the trouble to get involved. Meanwhile, outside there were playgrounds and a fun fair for the next generation of Jaguar men and women.

Concurrent with the September Trade launches, the Press were being flown up to Scotland for 'Ride & Drive'. Every couple of days a new batch would arrive to go through the routine. Following a flight to Edinburgh and collection by chauffeurs – a team of retired policemen – we were driven 70

149

odd miles to Dunkeld. We arrived in the evening at the excellent Stakis Dunkeld House Hotel and the presentation commenced. Following a video, a senior engineer ran through the salient points and the car was unveiled. Over champagne we examined the car and various displays with other company men. Following dinner we retired to prepare for the day ahead.

Meanwhile the Press are being treated to the delights of the XJ40 in Scotland; here Colin Cook, as every PR man should, bows to the product. (J.C.)

In an especially erected marquee beside the hotel, the Press cars are readied and checked after the ravages of the journalists. (J.C.)

After breakfast we were paired off and chose a car to try. An excellent route had been planned through the splendid countryside and over the deserted Scottish roads. After 90 miles we stopped at Kildrummy Castle, a delightful establishment, for coffee, and we changed cars. A further 125 miles through some of the most spectacular countryside in these isles took us back to the hotel and lunch.

Selecting another car we drove to Pitlochry and visited the smallest distillery in Scotland and thence back to the hotel. A superb dinner, complete with haggis piped in, followed and a little sampling of the myriad malts took place. Next morning the chauffeurs

Colin Cook and Val West, in light coloured anoraks, explain to a couple of journalists where they are! (J.C.)

The 'pride of achievement' was the banner under which the XJ40 was launched to the workforce and their families. (Cricket)

transported us back to reality – it's a hard life being a muttering rotter!

This went on for the whole month of September and I understand matters were enlivened by the journalist who tried to reverse through a narrow gateway with the doors open, the pair who tried to get a photograph of the car with all four wheels off the ground and the two Australian journalists who happened to be rally drivers and treated the route as a special stage!

For Colin Cook, of the PR department, it was a month of very hard work.

We actually started off at the end of August and we finally got away at the beginning of October. We entertained 400

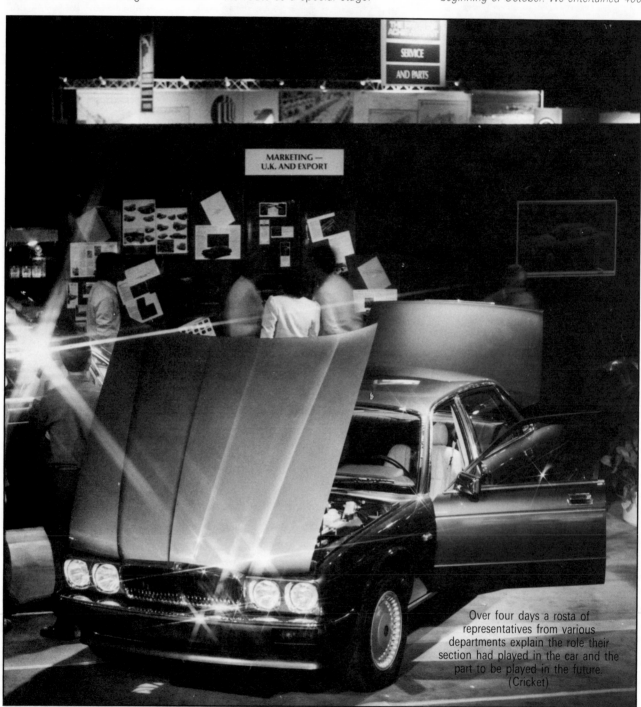

Over four days a rosta of representatives from various departments explain the role their section had played in the car and the part to be played in the future.
(Cricket)

journalists from all over the world – UK, Europe, USA, Canada, Australia and one from South Africa, who was on holiday in Scotland and just turned up!

Since the trade launches, states Chris Baker, we have done three further abbreviated reruns. On 1 October we did a launch for the City – stockbrokers, financiers, major City personalities, politicians, people of that ilk who either could not or would not come up to Coventry.

We did that at the Hilton. We took the three ton 'reveal' apparatus with us and had to have it set up 24 hours after it left the NEC. We topped and tailed the video with a little bit of Jaguar history. In fact it was the only time during the entire launch process that we permitted ourselves more than a passing reference to the great

Below: A very considerable amount of effort had gone into organising the 'J' Days with displays of running gear and components with various suppliers also represented. (Cricket)

Above: An XJ40, prepared for launch and demonstration to the UK police forces, is seen in the Manufacturing Assembly section. (Cricket)

sporting days. It seemed entirely appropriate to do that because clearly one of the major things we have to impact upon the City, is that the company that was so successful in the past, was a company that had evolved according to a carefully laid plan in terms of steady growth and consolidation.

We wanted to make the point to the City that that was how we saw the company progressing today. It certainly went down very well. You can get very cynical about these things but, for a British audience, they were as demonstrative and vocal as any we had seen.

To try to ensure that the people who measure our progress and our success in brutal economic and financial terms understood what we were doing, we had a preview for City analysts from the UK and

US, and a day for City editors and financial editors.

The City launch paid for itself when Lord Hanson apparently placed an order for no less than 100 cars!

However much planning you put in, inevitably something goes wrong. The XJ40 launch was no exception.

We had some wonderful heart-stopping moments, like losing 90 per cent of the power, five minutes before the start of the city launch. The Chairman was concerned when he heard somebody shout some jargon to the effect that they'd lost a phase of the power supply and he turned to me and said, 'what does "we've lost a phase" mean?'

I said, 'Basically, we've got a snag in the power supply but it's nothing very much'. He obviously thought that was all too glib an answer so he turned round to one of the production team and said, 'what does "we've lost a phase mean?" The chap turned round and said, 'that means you've got no f------ lights, sir!'

That was not quite the degree of frankness I had in mind at that precise moment!

This brings us up to 7 October during the evening of which most dealers around the UK staged a launch party prior to the official launch to the public-at-large next day. A senior manager from Jaguar attended each event.

'In exactly the same way that when, frankly, the going was bloody hard, when we were right at the bottom of the hole in 1980/81, one of the things we did was mobilise all our senior managers in a series of roadshows and we got ourselves out to talk to the dealers and the customers to say there is life after death, we are listening, we are concerned to get it right.

It seemed that when you had good news,

to send people out again to represent the company was a very fair counterbalance. I don't yet know how many people attended these events, but I can tell you that the dealers ordered a total of 120,000 tickets to send out.

I attended the party at Colliers in Sutton Coldfield and imagine the format was similar around the country. After liquid refreshment, we were ushered into the spotless workshops which were in darkness. Following what seemed like an eternity, no doubt to heighten the effect, broken only by

On 7 October dealers around the country held parties to launch the car and here we see Colliers celebrating with General Manager, Mike Roberts, second from the left, Alan Clark, Colliers Group Chairman on his left and, opposite him, Paul Stokes from Jaguar. (Colliers)

emotive music, short speeches set the scene and amid much dry ice and lighting effects, the ramps, whose tops had been screened off, were lowered and cars with headlamps blazing emerged from the artificial fog.

It was all good theatre and produced the desired result as the sharp intaking of breath and the 'oohs' and 'aahs' all around testified.

'They were very, very successful,' reports Robert Collier (who has no connection with the garage mentioned above). 'The response was very high and a number of people ordered cars. A lot of dealers then went into the next two or three days with demonstrations and follow-up events for additional people. Some of our dealers were giving 80 or 90 demonstrations a day! Guy Salmon did 80 in a few hours on the Wednesday. I was there on the Thursday and in two hours they did 50, with five cars on the go!'

On 8 October the car was officially unleashed on the public and what has been described as 'the industry's best known secret' was finally secret no longer. A few days later the Birmingham Motor Show opened and once again, just as Sir William and Bill Heynes had done so many times in the past, Jaguar had once again 'stolen the show'.

Significantly, the Jaguar stand was stylish but simple. Not for them all the expensive fancy chrome tubular or black girdering that made up other stands. The car was the star of Jaguar's stand, not the stand. Encouragingly,

'firm' enquiries numbered nearly three times the 1984 level.

Roger Putnam sums up all the effort. 'We are a very tiny company and we have to make every pound do a lot more than some of the volume manufacturers do. What we lack in budget, we make up for in personal human resource input and imagination. It's one of the most significant events that Jaguar will go through, probably this decade. As such we are determined to match the car's performance with our own.'

Chapter 10
Reflections

The turn-round has been remarkable. If one had been writing of Jaguar in the mid-seventies, one would have had little, if anything, to look forward to with the Ryder Report's effective intention of submerging the identity of one of Britain's proudest names. Now a little more than ten years later, the company is independent, healthy and has a widely acclaimed saloon to worry the competition and take the company into the nineties with its proud feline head leaping high.

Above all, there is now much to look forward to. The excitement generated by the XKs and the E-types seems a long time ago, but Jim Randle and Geof Lawson, with what Derek Wael-end calls Geof's 'dream factory', are working to recreate that excitement. Instead of merely having a famous past, Jaguar now has a future as well.

We have developments in all areas that you would expect a company such as us to have [states Randle]. We have turbo charger developments, traction control developments, and four-wheel drive devel-

opments. As we have developed our engineering ability, so we have expanded into areas of research that otherwise would have been denied us. We have a toe in most departments now.

The truth is that Jaguar has a unique style and it requires people who are sympathetic to that style. XJ40 benefitted from Sir William's influence.

As the years went by and we moved away from BL, his interest in the company grew again and I used to see him a great deal. He'd be in here at least once a month, and usually once a fortnight, to help us with this car and the next car, and the next car – they've all got his influence. He's passed some of it on to me. I hope, and certainly some on to Geof Lawson. So we hope to keep the traditions going.

We spoke of the original Italian styling offerings. 'You have to understand the sort of features that make a Jaguar car, a Jaguar car. I don't think people outside the company readily recognise that.'

I pressed Jim to be more specific as

to how the Grand Old Man had contributed.

It was usually small details. He would come and look at it and say, 'No, Randle. Stand over here, I don't think that looks quite right, do you?' And I would say, 'Oh, well, I suppose you're right,' and change it. We used to argue quite frequently about the motor car. He never actually said, 'Do this'. He always said, 'Do you think that's quite right?' Usually when you went away and thought about it for a while you would agree with him.

He certainly hadn't lost his touch, or his mental capacity. I loved that man dearly, I must say.

I miss him now. But he left a good legacy. Those of us who can stay the pace will try to keep it going. Certainly the next three cars that you will see, will still have Sir William's influence.

The man who is given the greatest credit for restoring Sir William's company to the height of former glories is, of course, John Egan whose efforts were recognised and rewarded, like

Jaguar's two knights, Sir John Egan and the late Sir William Lyons, are seen surrounded by shining armour. (J.C.)

those of Jaguar's founder, with a knighthood in 1986.

Egan is a straightforward, straight talking man who is refreshingly free of frills and respected for his readiness to be seen by, and chat to, the man on the shopfloor. Everybody one speaks to in Jaguar is adamant that the company owes its existence, and they owe their job, to Egan.

In effect he was the first full-time Chairman Jaguar had had since Lofty England's sadly premature departure and the first to be totally committed to the company in the same way. He took over Bob Knight's dogged, and immeasurably vital, fight for Jaguar's identity and independence within the gargantuan empire, one might say vampire.

John Morgan, talking of Egan, recalls that, 'it was only through his fighting that we kept production of the 'S' going. It would have been stopped. John Egan said to me, 'Come on, we're going up to Bickenhill (BL offices), we're going to give them hell.' He said to them, 'I've been reading this report, I don't think you know what you're talking about. I just do not believe the market has gone'.

In 1986 the XJS production accounted for a figure approaching a third of total production of around 40,000 cars; and the talk of Jaguar being a one make company often overshadows the important role played by this model.

'In '81 he said to me, 'We must become independent of this lot'.

'The way he treated them at meetings, my goodness, I used to cringe. He said to me, 'I know you hate coming to these meetings with me but we've got to go and do it'. I used to sit there and he'd attack – did he attack them! I could see them all thinking, 'God, what are we going to do with this man?' Apart from Sir Michael Edwardes, who

Sir John Egan poses with a piece of Jaguar's heritage, a fabulous long-nose D type, once described as the world's longest running advert. (J.C.)

I think he admired considerably, he tore a number of them to shreds!'

A good deal of the Chairman's job is as his company's frontman, concentrating, if you like, on Public Relations; and with David Boole's assistance, Egan has done a masterly job marketing himself and Jaguar. It is not all so public though, as this anecdote of John Morgan's illustrates.

John recalls the days when the directors of firms like Triumph and Rover had lunch served to them by butlers. Of course Sir William, whose reputation for thrift is now fondly remembered, would have none of this sort of thing. 'In Sir William's day it was a sort of one and sixpenny lunch from Joe Lyons that they would do under contract! It was quite adequate though and all directors and executives would sit together, which was a tremendous advantage, because it enabled us to converse on a wide range of the company's activities.'

When during part of the BL era, Morgan was doubling up as a Triumph Director, he discovered how other companies behaved. It did not please Lofty England who would say to him, 'I know why you like to go down there, Dai. It's because you get served by a butler!'
Morgan continues:

They used to invite various VIP's to lunch and I learnt that that was a good thing to do. When I came back here, we used to invite all the people who we felt could influence opinion, not only Press people, but people from the city – bankers, for example. We made lists of people we thought were VIP's in London. One of the great problems of the Midlands, I've always thought, is that they never appreciated that the money for our industry comes from London and that the general image of anything can be made or broken in the City, and around Westminster.

I realised that was how Lord Stokes had become the boss of the British motor industry in the sixties and I realised how Lord Rootes had done it, in my previous life with that company, by his connections in

the City and in politics.

It was fascinating entertaining all these people. One day we had a gentleman called Lord Khadoori of Hong Kong, who was one of our biggest customers for Daimler limousines in the Far East. He'd just placed an order for £800m with General Electric for a complete new power station and was over to collect his title. We asked him if he would like to come up and have a look at our new Jaguar factory.

'I'd arranged with some caterers to bring us in some pork pies, scotch eggs and some bits of lettuce on tin plates covered with plastic wrapping,' recalls Morgan with much merriment. 'We got some cheap 'vin de table' stuff and when he arrived Sir John asked him if he'd like a sherry. So I poured him a sherry and said, 'would you like to sit here, sir, next to John Egan and we'll just get serving'.

I took the plastic covering off, made him a salad and plonked it down in front of him whilst John served himself. We were just about to sit down when John said, 'Of course, I haven't really introduced you, or do you already know John Morgan, my Sales Director?'

So Kadoori said, 'No, I don't think I do'.

Well, this is John Morgan, 'said John Egan.

Oh,' he said, 'it's you, is it?'

So I said, 'Yes, I think you thought I was the butler, didn't you?'

He was so taken aback he said, 'Yes, I did!'

John said to him, 'We don't have anything like that here, Lord Khadoori'.

Those were the days – everything was done by hand as it were. You have to build the image as well as the car, and that, I think, has always been Jaguar's force.'

Ken Edwards has worked very closely with Egan in the last few years on the Personnel side and as Company Secretary.

I think the most important thing has been the construction of the new company. If you remember, in 1980 we were still part of BL and, therefore, a lot of the services were still centralised and we had to build up our company so that, when we moved into

privatisation, we were able to do these things ourselves and not rely on any company outside. So that has been the biggest problem, that and building up a strong enough management team to lead the company forward.

We have to compete against two of the finest companies in the world – Mercedes and BMW – from a management point of view, and so we really had to match our style and set our sights at the same level.

Regarding the workforce, I think the biggest problem has been moving them from a demotivated group, which I think they were in the BL days where they felt that they couldn't influence anything themselves, to engender pride in the company again, and in their work. We have also striven to move them financially from being in the lower 'quartile' of the wages league up to the highest 'quartile,' but to do it in such a way that we could finance this

from productivity. And now we've done it.

They are now the highest paid workforce in the British motor car industry. Their productivity has increased threefold.

Communication is the secret. I've always felt that communication was the selling arm of personnel. It's explaining to the workforce and management what we are trying to do, what the problems are and how we intend to tackle them. It's also listening to them, finding out what suggestions they have to make, because really what we are trying to do is harness all their energy so that we can move forward, and that's the secret.

Perhaps not surprisingly, in view of the parlous state of the company, John Egan did not immediately jump at the chance of becoming Jaguar Chairman but instead deliberated for some four months.

I knew that the company was losing an awful lot of money. I knew that there was a great deal of friction between the employees of Jaguar and BL. I also knew the cars weren't very satisfactory in terms of quality and reliability as I had one of my own at the time.

I was also concerned about an even deeper problem. Was it still possible to make cars in the United Kingdom? Was it possible to actually do it, or had labour relations and people's will to win suffered so much that it wasn't even possible?

So in a way, one had to try and wrestle with all those kind of problems, before one could come to a conclusion that it was actually worth having a go. In the end I decided to give it some time. I had a Series II and had a look at a Series III, which I believed answered what I thought were the major customer criticisms of the Series II. I felt it was a very beautiful development, well organised, well thought out and I thought it's probably just worth it, just to see if it is possible.

I thought there was probably just over a fifty per cent chance of survival, and I gave it a go.

In those days there was little demand for the product. The dealers all had plenty of cars in stock and they were having to

discount them heavily to sell them. The production processes were extremely unproductive, so it really was in quite a mess. However we chose quality as the number one problem to attack and it has been well chronicled how we went through quality and timing and productivity. We looked very carefully at our customers and dealerships.

We've done a tremendous job on developing our dealerships. I think in particular the job they've done in the UK is really quite remarkable when you think that we had hardly any Jaguar dealerships really worth anything four years ago, and I think at the time of the launch of XJ40, we had 71 solus or near solus Jaguar sites – a

tremendous achievement, not only for our own staff but our dealerships.

Then of course there was the building up of a technology base, the building up of an organisation capable of designing and developing new world class cars which has meant building up an Engineering department of over a thousand people from one that originally had only 250 people.

The Jaguar Board is seen here, as it was at the time of privatisation and is today with the exception that Roger Putnam has taken the place of Neil Johnson (standing third from left) as Sales & Marketing Director. On Sir John Egan's left is Graham Whitehead, President of Jaguar Inc. in the States and Chairman of Jaguar Canada. (J.C.)

So that was the sort of programme. Amongst all that was the general notion that we would need a car to follow Series III and the subject was already started when I arrived here. In fact, I think the XJ40 clay had already been signed off before I arrived. People knew what the car was supposed to be and a great many of

the parameters were already decided upon. My task at the time was to get acceptance by the BL Board, and as it turned out by the Government as well, that the project was a viable one and that a hundred million pounds was worth gambling on the project.

The difficulty I had as a businessman at the time, even then, was to look at the business with a turnover of only about

I enquired of Sir John if he ever really believed he was not going to make it.

Things got so desperate between September/October 1980 and June/July '81, that you didn't so much think of the longer term. We planned out what we thought was a good atttack on the long term, but you really had to fight your battles day-by-day, because there were battles to be fought every day.

I have heard stories that Sir Michael Edwardes had actually given orders that Jaguar must close. Was this true or apochryphal?

Well, I have since heard from one or two Cabinet Ministers that there was a great

£150m which was losing forty odd million pounds, and asking for £100m to invest in a new car! There is no question it was a great act of faith on behalf of the BL Board and the Government in giving me the money to go ahead and have a go.

I think, however, by the time they had to decide, roughly early in '81, there were already glimmerings of light beginning to appear, and certainly by August of '81 the turn-around had very definitely started. I think we broke even, or even made a slight profit in that month and from January 1982 onwards we have been in profit since.

David Boole, as Director of Communications and Public Affairs, which is more traditionally known as PR, has worked to rebuild the Jaguar image and drive home the quality message. (J.C.)

deal of worry that the financial performance of the company was so bad that it was requiring so much money that the only sensible thing to do would be to close it down. So it was very definitely an item for consideration. I think maybe we've been a bit of a lucky company in many ways, and

perhaps there was an element of luck for some time, but we managed to get through. Indeed I've often said to everybody that it was a bit of a Houdini act.

XJ40, in those dark days in 1981, did represent hope for the future when a lot of people could never have dreamt that we could make a successful company based on the existing Series III. So the timing of the programme for XJ40 was a big symbol of hope to everybody. If we could only grapple with the size of the problems that we were currently tackling, if we could develop this new car, there was a future beyond that.

It is said that BL felt the XJ saloons were not selling simply because they were old fashioned and hence the creation of the more Germanic, box-like early styling exercises.

There was a great deal of thought, particularly probably in BL Technology, that the Jaguar was an old-fashioned car and you could never really sell it. I never believed that. I always felt that it did have world class roadholding and that it was very beautiful. I think, by the way, we did a lot of detailed improvement to the car, particularly on the interior.

I never thought a classic shape like that could be old-fashioned.

Next we talked about the part Sir John has played in the XJ40 project.

I think my role has been to try and work at the interface between the XJ project and the company, to make certain that I felt sure that at each stage the company was capable of doing the next phase of the project, that we had indeed an Engineering department capable of developing the car, that we had testing routines capable of testing whether the car had achieved the levels it should do, of making sure that we had a testing routine that told us we were safe to move on to the next stage each time.

There was one very absurd statement made by one union official, who said that the whole of the company was watching the Chairman playing roulette as to when, or when not, to launch the XJ40. It was an

immensely naïve and insulting remark, in that we had evolved a very careful programme of evaluation of the prototype, and later, on the early production cars, all the components and the complete car in every environment we could possibly test it. We never really moved on to the next stage until we'd got each one right.

I also had to make sure the interface between Engineering and Manufacturing was working, and for that we built the Pilot Build Facility which made a complete communication process possible. I had to make sure we had rational and sane purchasing policies to ensure that we were buying from people who were capable of giving us the kind of quality that we wanted, and of course that we had an atmosphere of productivity and quality into which to put a new car.

Never expect a new thing to sweep all before it and get everything right. It won't get the environment right, you've got to make that right beforehand. Also we had to be sure that we had a Sales & Marketing department capable of a world class launch. You can have a lovely car and just mess up the relationships with the media and with the dealers and the public. And then of course we had to have dealers capable of dealing with the product.

I think four or five years ago the product would have been wasted on a very amateurish set of dealers. I think the dealers we have now, for example the UK dealers, have done a superbly professional job in selling out the previous XJ6. I don't think I heard of a single XJ6 discounted. There were certainly hardly any left when we launched the XJ40.

Egan, like his colleagues, stresses that Jaguar never really had a firm date for the launch and so it was not a matter of putting the date back. Above all the car has to be right and even in that last year there was still much to be done.

> When Sir John joined, the Series III was in production but beset by poor reliability as a result of inferior component quality and painting, but he set about the problems with single-minded zeal building on the efforts initiated by Bob Knight. (J.C.)

What didn't we do? We looked at everything. We had to change over our paint technology, complete our engine refinement programme, beat 'Gas Guzzler' in the States, finish off our refinement process – we knew we had got superb roadholding but we needed the ride to go with it, and we wanted to improve upon an already very good performer in XJ6. We wanted to put all the wood, chrome and old world charm into the interior.

Originally it was a very plastic interior which was very much modelled upon what we called luxury cars. Our competitors Mercedes-Benz and BMW had an almost complete plastic interior and we had wood, leather and chrome, and we thought that was old fashioned. When we had a clinic, as long ago as February, 1984, we discovered the best and most highly thought of competitor of all was Series III! So we worked very, very hard putting the old world charm back into the XJ40, and I think we managed to do it in a very dashing, modern use of those beautiful old materials.

I changed the subject entirely and asked Sir John for his views on motor sport and whether an involvement was benefitting the company.

Both of our racing programmes are in pretty good shape. Obviously you can't win all the time but we've done a fair bit of winning. In a way, Jaguar is expected to go racing and is expected to be competitive. One of the things that does concern me, however, about racing, is the instability of the rules and regulations which do mitigate against really spending any money on it.

But we have enjoyed our racing and I think it has reflected well on the company. The racing programmes have put some money back into our 'image bank'.

Changing the subject again totally, in these times of volatile relationships between national currencies and Jaguar's emphasis on export, and in particular to the US, currency fluctuations could make Jaguar very unstable.

We make the car in pounds, and get the

The Chairman hosts the City at the Hilton launch of the XJ40 and discusses one of Britain's finest companies with the Hon. Alan Clark, Minister of Trade. Following an early career with Bahrain Petroleum and Shell International, Egan moved to the motor industry joining, first, General Motors and then BL, for whom he set up the Unipart operation. From Unipart Egan moved, in 1975, to Massey Ferguson with the responsibility for its European parts operations until tempted to join Jaguar as Chairman in 1980, becoming also Managing Director in 1982. (J.C.)

cash in dollars. So we decided the first thing we wanted was stability. We therefore hedged, or sold forward, the majority of our receivables on a rolling twelve month basis. Later on we amended that policy to say that whenever we saw a particularly good exchange rate, we would go further out. Then we finished off by amending the policy even further by adding in the possibility of options, which allow you to some extent to cut off your losses and exploit good exchange rates if they occur.

So we've got a fairly sophisticated view now of trying to balance stability against doing well with good exchange rates and cutting off our losses with bad exchange rates. Up till now it has worked very well bringing great stability into the company and enabling us to do some pretty long range planning.

We have of course an immense amount

of money to invest. There was very little money invested in the 1970s nor did we have, until very recently, a Production Engineering department capable of spending these vast sums of money. The very first major investment year was 1986 and we spent the best part of £100m. This year it will be even more, but it took four years to build up a Production Engineering department capable of spending that amount of money wisely.

Playing devil's advocate I asked whether such competitive pricing was a wise policy when, at the time of talking, XJ40 delivery was six months and rising.

We take a pretty long term view of our business. We intend to develop over the relatively long term, continually growing, always keeping demand ahead of supply.

We also have, now, very impressive resale values for our cars. This makes the cost of ownership of one of our cars very low and I think we give a pretty good package to the consumer.

Communication is, as Ken Edwards has said, of major importance to Jaguar with continual briefings, videos, study courses and such events as 'J' Day as witness to this. The strike following the announcement of the car was, though mercifully brief, sickeningly disappointing, being a reminder of the industrial evil of the strife-torn sixties and seventies. There is genuinely a splendid atmosphere at Jaguar today redolent of the Le Mans heydays of the fifties and the workforce seems to have rediscovered their spirit and commitment to the future. One just wonders whether their representatives truly represent that enthusiasm.

I doubt if I can see the major union, the Transport & General Workers union, ever becoming interested in the success of companies. They seem to be too politically motivated. They don't seem to think it matters whether companies are successful or not. It is an extraordinary view that I find very difficult to understand. But there is evidence that some of the other unions are beginning to become interested in the planning routines of companies, in training within companies and, indeed, some of them are beginning to do some very interesting training themselves.

I think, for example, that the Engineering Workers Union is taking a very interesting attitude towards helping companies to develop and certainly they've struck some very interesting agreements with companies, including new automobile companies in the UK. But for the moment the T & GW does not seem very interested in helping companies to develop. They seem not to have managed to go beyond demanding more money for doing less work, and as that's an insatiable direction, it's not constructive.

When Jaguar was split off from BL and floated as a separate company, a healthy proportion of employees took up the share schemes and took a stake in their company. I wondered if this had produced, or fostered, a sense of commitment.

People have got to try and take common cause with their employer. If they can't, in the end, the company will go out of business. I think our share scheme has helped to demonstrate to people that success is better than failure.

The majority of our employees have got something like £2,600 worth of shares. To many people this will be the most disposable money they've ever had in their lives. Bringing wealth to people isn't just bringing more money to their weekly wage packet. Giving them the security of a big solid bunch of money like that, I think, is a tremendous increase to the quality of their lives.

As to the future?

I think we should carry on doing the kind of things we've been doing – making better motor cars, satisfying more customers, developing our dealers, developing our technology base, and just becoming a better competitor.

There will be substantial exhancements of our product line every year from now on.

Finally I asked Sir John Egan what he, personally, liked about the XJ40.

I think with a Jaguar it has to have beauty, it has to have very good roadholding and refinement of ride, and it has to have good performance. Without these things, it is not a Jaguar.

There seems little doubt in the minds of the Press, the public, the dealers, the employees and Sir John, that the new XJ6s are every inch a Jaguar in the finest tradition of those eminent predecessors Sir William Lyons, William Heynes CBE, Lofty England and Bob Knight CBE plus their many colleagues over the years.

It is a tribute to them that the more recent team have had to strive so hard to better their standards. It is a tribute to their successors, Sir John Egan, Jim Randle and fellow Directors, and to every single Jaguar employee that they have so clearly succeeded, and produced a car worthy of the great name of Jaguar.

The legend lives on.

Index